Table of Contents

The opinions expressed in this report are the authors' and do not reflect the official positions of the U.S. Military Academy, the U.S. Army, the Department of Defense, the U.S. government, or any of the individuals or organizations that agreed to release information for this report.

Preface

In the years following the attacks of September 11, 2001, the Combating Terrorism Center (CTC) at West Point has extended significant effort to understand the ideologies, strategies, and structures that define terrorist groups, as well as the tactics and techniques they employ to inflict damage on their adversaries. As became painfully evident on 9/11, al-Qa'ida and its associated groups and networks—Sunni extremist movements—posed the most formidable terrorist threat to U.S. national security. For that reason, the CTC's research program has historically focused on Sunni militant groups.

The 17 July 2008 terrorist attacks on two hotels in Jakarta, Indonesia were a vivid reminder of the breadth of the battle space and the importance of constant vigilance. This break in Indonesia's four-year calm might be a one-time event or an indication of a resurgent regional terror threat. With crude weapons and little logistical support, a small group of people were capable of carrying out an attack that received global media attention. The focus on the perpetrators of this attack may also veil the importance of ideologies other than global jihadism to political violence in the region, such as various strands of ethno-nationalism. As this report highlights, global jihadism is not the only ideology animating terrorist violence, and ethno-nationalism is still a prevalent force in Southeast Asia.

The inherent difficulty of tactical defense makes it ever more important to address the broader ideological and strategic aspects of the terror threat in the hopes of identifying important trends. This volume examines the salience and content of jihadi ideology across Southeast Asia in an attempt to gain a better understanding of the types of threats and susceptibility to global jihadist violence in the region.

The volume continues the CTC tradition of trying to understand actors posing a real or potential threat to the United States and follows projects such as *The Militant Ideology Atlas* and *Cracks in the Foundation*. Edited by Dr. Scott Helfstein, this volume is an attempt to gain greater granularity on the nature of jihadism in Southeast Asia. The volume uses a country-based approach, focusing on jihadi ideology in Indonesia, Malaysia, Philippines, and Thailand. The final chapter looks at jihadi content on the internet. CTC hopes this report serves both the academic and practitioner communities to better understand the landscape of terrorism in Southeast Asia.

The Landscape of Jihadism in Southeast Asia

Scott Helfstein[1]

Introduction

With both secular and Islamic governments, Southeast Asia is often portrayed as a representative model of progressive Islam, while also suffering longstanding Muslim separatist conflicts. The region has been the target of numerous terrorist attacks over the past decade, but the character and motivation for these attacks varies widely. Many of these attacks are rooted in national or regional ethnic struggles, but others reflect the grander Salafi-Jihadi ambition of building a regional or global caliphate. A significant component of future discord and collaboration in the region is tied the nature of the populations' grievances and the trajectory of radical Islam. This report addresses the diffusion of jihadist thought in Southeast Asia, in the hope that understanding past and present jihadist trends in the region help minimize threats in the future.

This report shows that the differences among nations, groups, and grievances in Southeast Asia generate a complex patchwork that does not fit into a neat paradigm. There are important characteristics that distinguish the threats faced by each country in the region, as well as important interconnections that tie them together. Some countries in the region (such as the Philippines and Thailand) face local ethno-nationalist Islamic insurgencies rooted in colonial policies. The minority groups involved in these struggles fight for separation or autonomy from the existing political regimes that they perceive to be guilty of imposing discriminatory policies. Jihadi ideology is largely irrelevant to these conflicts, playing a minimal role in recruiting and morale building if it is present at all.

The affective impact of these local, ethno-nationalist conflicts, however, has regional consequences. Radical Islamist elements in other Southeast Asian nations (such as Malaysia and Indonesia) use these insurgencies to rally support for the Islamist agenda and radicalize those sympathetic to the plight of Muslim minorities elsewhere. In some cases, fundamentalists unleash their aggression against the foreign governments in the region opposing insurgent forces (i.e. Indonesian fighters in the Philippines). More often, however, these radicalized groups target their own government or global interests within their country in an

[1] I would like to thank Reid Sawyer and Dominick Wright for feedback on prior drafts. Any mistakes are my own.

attempt to further their cause of extremist interpretations of Islam and sharia jurisprudence. Jihadist literature is more prominent in these environments than those with longstanding ethno-nationalist grievances. Given the roots and motivations of different groups, this discrepancy is not surprising, but the fluid nature of the Southeast Asian political landscape complicates any attempt to simplify or categorize grievances. Extensive ties among certain radical groups suggest that there is a great deal of ideological cross-fertilization, though they manifest in unique ways due to the significant differences among the extremist elements in different countries.

The remainder of this introduction highlights several convergent and divergent forces among the countries and groups within the region to set the stage for the detailed case studies that follow. The volume is largely organized along geographic lines, with chapters examining the influence of jihadist thinking in Indonesia, Malaysia, The Philippines, and Thailand. Each chapter outlines the ideological roots of key insurgent and terrorist groups, as well as the jihadi influence on these groups given personal relationships and jihadist literature translated into local languages. The final chapter looks at an increasingly important distribution platform for jihadist ideas now and for the future, the Internet, examining some of the major websites in various languages in an attempt to shed some light on ideological characteristics of jihadis in Southeast Asia.

The Nature of Violence and Jihadi Ideology

There are different ways one might classify or categorize the terrorist violence across Southeast Asian countries. According to the Worldwide Incidents Tracking System (WITS) maintained by the National Counter Terrorism Center, from 2004 to May 2009 Thailand experienced 3301 incidents, the Philippines 1061, Indonesia 148, and Malaysia 15.[2] By this measure, the conflicts in Thailand and the Philippines are the most active in the region, but the analysis in this volume shows that they are least influenced by global jihadi ideology. Further analysis of those attacks from the WITS database shows there are Islamic connections to 4% (144) of attacks in Thailand, 9% (95) in the Philippines, 8% (12) in Indonesia, and 20% (3) in Malaysia. This data illustrates that violence is quite high in Thailand and the Philippines relative to Malaysia and Indonesia, but the majority of incidents in the first two countries are more directly tied to ethno-

---

[2] Note that these results were produced by searching for the total number of attacks in each country, then limiting the country search to attacks coded as having Sunni-religious motivations.

nationalist aims rather than a globally focused religious motivation. It would wrong, however, to simply assume there is a straightforward inverse relationship between global jihadi ideology and violence in Southeast Asia.

Conflicts in the Philippines and Thailand have a distinctly local character, more separatist or ethno-nationalist in nature than religious. Conflict in the Christian majority Philippines has focused on the southern territories of Mindanao, Tawi-Tawi, Basilan, and the Sulu Archipelago. The poor economic conditions in this region have convinced the Muslim majority that Islamic government would better serve them.[3] Since the fighting began in the 1970s, violence has ebbed and flowed, resulting in the deaths of 100,000 people in Mindanao alone.[4] Over time, Muslim resistance has splintered with some groups demanding autonomy and others calling for independence. For example, the Moro National Liberation Front (MNLF) abandoned their call for independence in favor of autonomy, and more radical members broke off to create the Moro Islamic Liberation Front (MILF), which continues to demand independence. The only groups that could be classified as jihadist, Abu Sayyaf Group (ASG) and the Raja Solaiman Movement (RSM), were offshoots of these separatist groups. Many Muslims view the Philippine conflict as a legitimate jihad, but inside the country jihad largely serves to create a common Moro-Muslim identity.

The main proponents of violence in the Philippines, the MNLF and the MILF, have linked with supporters from the Middle East at different times, but any discussion of jihad is primarily used as a mobilizing tool for the local ethnic campaign. There are, however, two groups in the Philippines that deviate from this pattern: ASG and the offshoot RSM. The beginnings of ASG trace back to training camps in Afghanistan during the 1980s. In 1987, Abdurajak Abubakar Janjalani traveled to Pakistan and made contact with Osma bin Laden, Abdur Rab Rasul Sayaaf, and Ramzi Yousef. The experience introduced Janjalani to jihadist ideology, and motivated him to start a jihadist group in the Philippines. From its inception, ASG defined itself according to its ethnic Moro identity, but its goals extended further than indepedence. There is limited penetration of jihadi literature evidenced by the availability of Abdullah Azzam's writings. After rapid growth in the mid-1990s, ASG and its small offshoot RSG began to deteriorate into criminal organizations. They remain marginalized players in the Philippine conflict.

---

[3] Note that the government has initiated different programs to improve conditions in these areas, but the programs have generated mixed results.

[4] Zachary Abuza, *Militant Islam in Southeast Asia* (London, UK: Lynne Reinner, 2003), p. 33.

The conflict in Thailand has similar characteristics to the Philippine conflict. While the majority of Thai are Buddhist, there is a Muslim majority in the southern provinces of Yala, Pattani, and Narathiwat. These territories are also among the poorest in Thailand, and the major employer is rubber plantations.[5] Recent actions by the government, including new economic development programs, an education plan expected to cost $90 million, and deployment of 20,000 troops to stabilize the region, have worked to reduce the severity of violence.[6] Nonetheless, the resistance remains active.

Jihadist ideology plays even less of a role in Thailand, where the Malay-Muslim militants in the southern provinces are largely driven by local grievances. Unlike the Philippines, Thailand has not seen the emergence of groups driven by global jihadist ideas such as ASG. Given the external support for the Malay-Muslims, one cannot completely discount the possibility that jihadi ideology has penetrated the region, but current evidence suggests it is unlikely. Much like MILF, notions of jihad are largely invoked to mobilize and recruit local fighters. Even the notion of jihad used by the Thai Muslims has a distinctly local character.

Muslims in Malaysia do not have minority grievances, and currently, there is no domestic insurgency in Malaysia. Muslims represent the majority of Malaysia's population, Islamic political parties and actors are permitted within government, and the tacit acceptance of radical elements in the past, seems to have immunized Malaysia from the violence experienced elsewhere in the region. While the Kumpulan Militan Malaysia (KMM) have conducted a few attacks targeting minority groups in Malaysia, those attracted to extremist ideology are motivated by regional and international issues. Many Malays sympathize with Muslims fighting in the Philippines and Thailand, as well as those in Palestine and other places. This sympathetic environment attracted international radical groups such as al-Qa'ida and Jemaah Islamiya (JI), who saw Malaysia as an ideal place to handle their logistical affairs. The importance these organizations placed on their safe haven reduced the incentive to target the moderately Islamic Malay government. Recently, however, the Malaysian government has increased its focus on radical elements, dismantling the local JI and KMM cells in the west, although the eastern part of the country remains a concern.

---

[5] Like the Philippines, the government has made efforts to improve conditions in these provinces.
[6] Jean Prajak, Speech given at the 2008 International Counterterrorism Conference, held at the Interdisciplinary Center, Herziliya, Israel.

Extremist Islam in Malaysia is a relatively recent phenomenon. The modern nation-state of Malaysia was born in 1957 with a largely secular government applying sharia law to matters of custom. The ostensibly moderate community slowly grew more Islamist in the late 1970s (corresponding with the Iranian Revolution, the Soviet invasion of Afghanistan, and the siege of the Grand Mosque). At the same, radical elements associated with Darul Islam (an unsanctioned Islamic party that turned violent) fled Indonesia for Malaysia, and received residency status. These individuals would use Malaysia as a base of operations. While there is a wide variety of jihadi material translated and made available in Malaysia, there is little evidence to suggest that it has generated a strong indigenous jihadi movement. Most recruits serve logistical purposes for foreign groups operating in Malaysia or received training for deployment elsewhere.

Conflict in Indonesia has both local and regional aspects. Indonesia's secular government, which prohibited the political participation of Islamic groups, became a target for locally motivated radicals demanding a greater role for sharia law. Groups like Darul Islam, and Dewan Dakwah Islamiyah Indonesia (DDII) fought domestically for the Islamic cause. These groups then generated the more radical, and more globally focused JI, which carried out a rash of high profile attacks against tourist destinations and international political targets from 1999 to 2005. There is no full-fledged conflict or insurgency as in the Philippines, but Indonesia is not immune to targeting the way Malaysia has been. At the same time, radical groups in Indonesia have a regional and global focus similar to those in Malaysia. Together, this combination continues to make Indonesia both a terrorist target and fertile recruitment ground.

This report shows that the Islamist movement in Indonesia is strongly rooted in early Islamist and jihadist thinking; it is therefore not surprising that Indonesian radical groups have the closest ties with the global jihadi movement. Muhammadiyah, now considered a legitmate religious outlet by the Indonesian government, was deeply influenced by Wahabi Puritanism during its founding in the early 20th century. The group's leaders were inspired by the writings of Hassan al-Banna, founder of the Muslim Brotherhood, and the ideas of the Abul Ala Maududi, and Indian cleric widely cited in jihadist literature. While Muhammadiyah became a non-violent Islamist activist group operating in the civil sphere, more radical and militant groups such as Persataun Islam and (DDII) also emerged over time. The Leadership of Persataun Islam was heavily influenced by Sayyid Qutb, and DDII leadership travelled to the Middle East. These more radical groups acted as precursor for JI. The two ideological leaders of JI, Abu Bakar Ba'asyir and Abdullah Sungkar, have connections with al-Qa'ida and sent a number of Indonesians and Malaysians to train in Afghan camps during the 1980s and 1990s.

Complex Interconnections

While this report deals with countries individually, there are important connections that weave throughout the volume. One example is Malaysia's history as a logistical hub and safe haven for extremist groups. Indonesian based JI only began to thrive after Malaysia provided safe haven for its two leaders Ba'asyir and Sungkar. During that time Ba'asyir and Sungkar radicalized and trained Malaysians, established a JI cell in Malaysia, and contributed to the development of the Malaysian KMM. At the same time, JI leadership was able to extend the structure of a terrorist group that would operate in Indonesia for fifteen years. In this way, terrorism in Malaysia and Indonesia is interconnected.

This temporary safe haven is not the only interconnection in the region. Many of the groups used common training facilities. During the 1980s, hundreds of Indonesians and Malaysians went to Pakistan and Afghanistan to fight the jihad, linking them together and exposing them to people from other regions with varying ideological perspectives. After the Afghan War, JI operatives then began training at the MILF's Abu Bakar facility in the Philippines. This common experience ties the Indonesian JI and Malaysian KMM to the Philippine MILF and ASG, facilitating cooperation. The only group that appears largely unconnected by training is the Malay-Muslims in Thailand.

Beyond these concrete relationships, radicalism in the region has more ephemeral interconnections in the hearts and minds of different populations. While the Thai Malay-Muslims have the weakest connections to other groups, the conflict still serves as motivation for Malaysians much as the Philippine conflict does. This sympathy translates to active or passive support for insurgencies and terror groups. The general ideas that underlay jihadi ideology, such as the creation of an Islamic state, have the ability to graft onto local grievances. Even in arenas largely devoid of jihadi literature, the core notion of jihad resonates; therefore, groups motivated by local grievances still maintain some connection to jihadi ideas. Further, the narrative and local grievances that drive the demand for an Islamic state, bolsters the status of and helps legitimize jihadi ideology. These ideological interconnections will prove the most difficult to address into the future.

Content Summary

The first article, by Rohan Gunaratna, examines the state of jihadi ideology in Malaysia. Gunaratna offers a historical account of Malay jihadism, then looks at some of the literature currently available. The historical account shows that Malaysia has a complicated relationship with Islamism in both the social and political spheres. His analysis concludes that Malaysia may continue to serve as a staging area for terrorists to coordinate future attacks. He also notes that the geopolitical characteristics of Malaysia means that counterterrorism efforts will confront substantively different threats in the eastern and western parts of the country.

In the second article, Greg Barton traces the roots of Islamism and jihadism in Indonesia. The article follows the development of radical Islamic groups in Indonesia, showing how increasingly radical elements grew out of more moderate predecessors. Barton also illustrates that the attempts to keep Islamist entities out of politics and confined to the social realm, may have inadvertently fueled support for Islamist forces. Indonesian jihadis have not produced much innovative material, but they have borrowed and blended from a number of sources to create a patchwork that resonates locally. He concludes that support for jihadist violence in Indonesia is limited, but more substantial than one might expect.

Renato Cruz de Castro addresses the state of jihadi ideology in the Philippines, specifically looking at ASG and RSM. He focuses on the influence of the Afghan jihad on Philippine experience, noting the historical absence of global jihadist ideology in the long-running Moro ethno-nationalist campaign. A small committed group of individuals returned from the Afghan jihad committed to the ideas of Usama bin Laden and those around him. Over time, the groups' behavior came to resemble a criminal element rather than a jihadi one, and al-Qa'ida withdrew their support. He argues that jihadism has not permeated the Philippines in any significant way, and the material that is available dates back to Sayyid Qutb and Abdullah Azzam.

The diffusion of jihadi ideology in Thailand remains limited according to Joseph Chinyong Liow. Thailand's Malay-Muslims focus on local grievances, though there is limited use of jihadi material to legitimize the local struggle and generate support. Liow examines the sources that generate this material, its content, and its importance. The limited quantity of jihadi literature found is often copied or paraphrased in pamphlets focused on the insurgency.

In the final article, Jarret Brachman surveys Southeast Asian jihadi material on the internet. The majority of this material comes from Indonesia, with less from

Malaysia and Thailand. He notes that these websites are structurally different from the popular Arabic language jihadi sites. The Arabic sites often use interactive web forums where individuals post and reply to messages. The Southeast Asian websites are either professional looking information providers or amateurish blogs. Brachman also notes that much of the material available is translated from English language jihadi sites rather the popular online Arabic forums. This shows great diversity in capability and a counterintuitive source of inspiration amongst jihadis in Southeast Asia.

The Current and Emerging Extremist Threat in Malaysia

Rohan Gunaratna

Introduction

Unlike those from most Southeast Asian countries, Malaysian Muslims become vulnerable to extremist ideologies due to international compulsions, rather than domestic grievances. Muslims in Malaysia are galvanized by the perception that Muslims are persecuted in southern Thailand, the southern Philippines, and eastern Indonesia as well as areas outside the Southeast Asia such as Palestine, Lebanon, Chechnya, Afghanistan, Iraq, and other conflict zones. Due to a deep sense of loyalty to their country, Malysian extremists are reluctant to mount attacks in Malaysia. However, their deep anger over the plight of Muslims around the world motivates a number of Malaysians to provide moral, logistical, and financial support to Islamic extremist groups, and some have even been willing to carry out terrorist attacks outside of Malaysia.

Over the past decade, the primary threat groups operating in Malaysia – including al-Qa'ida, al-Jama'a al-Islamiyya (JI), Darul Islam (DI), and Kumpulan Militan Malaysia (KMM) – have been formally dismantled. Nonetheless, some members, sympathizers, and supporters have organized themselves into cells or linked up with other extremist groups. At the same time, a new generation of Malaysian radicals is being groomed both at home and abroad. Groups espousing radical ideologies such as Hizbut Tahrir remain active in Malaysia. Like the Indonesian government, the Malaysian government is reluctant to outlaw such "conveyer belt" groups not directly linked to violence, but espouse radical perspectives that may help to justify violence. Furthermore, a sizeable number of radical foreign ideologues, preachers, and financiers from the region and beyond continue to visit Malaysia, and a few hundred Malaysian students are studying in radical madaris in Indonesia, Pakistan, and elsewhere.

Given the threat that Malaysia poses as a source of support for foreign extremists and operatives willing to engage in violence in neighboring countries, this chapter explores Malaysia's relationship with Islamist extremism over the past three decades and how it will continue in the near future. The piece demonstrates that while Malaysia represents a model for Southeast Asian countries in terms of combating the operational threat posed by Islamic extremists, the country must remain vigilant against an ongoing threat of ideological extremism.

The Rise of Islamist Extremism in Malaysia: 1980s – 1990s

Ideological Foundations of the Rise in Islamic Extremism

Malaysia did not exist as a unified state until 1957; prior to that time, the region consisted of a multiple British colonies established in the late 18th Century. Under colonial rule, few Malaysian organizations were structured along religious lines: among those that were, the most notable were *Parti Orang Muslimin Malaya (Hizbul Muslimin)*, founded in 1948, and Islamic Party of Malaysia (PAS), founded in 1951.[1] Although certain leaders used the language of jihad in the Malaysia's fight for independence,[2] the newly established state largely embraced the secular system adopted by the colonial rulers.[3] Specifically, the vision for Malaysia espoused by Tunku Abdul Rahman, the first Prime Minister of Malaysia (1957 – 1970), was a secular State with Islam as the official religion.[4] Islamic law (*Shari'ah*) was applied in affairs of custom, but its interpretation remained restricted to peripheral matters concerning personal and family matters.[5]

Despite the moderate foundations of the country, Islamic revivalism began to take root in Malaysia in the late 1970s, a trend that continued throughout the 1980s and 1990s. While partly the product of domestic politicians seeking to play the "Muslim card" to capture and sustain political power,[6] the growth of Islamic extremism during this time was largely tied to international events that affected Muslim communities worldwide, including the 1979 Iranian Revolution, the Soviet invasion of Afghanistan (1979-1989), the siege of the Grand Mosque in

---

[1] Farish Noor, *Islam Embedded: The Historical Development of the Pan-Malaysian Islamic Party PAS (1951 - 2003)*, (Kuala Lumpur: MSRI, 2004).

[2] Kevin K. Birth, "Reading and the Righting of Writing Ethnographies," *American Ethnologist* 17, no. 3 (August 1990), 539; Moshe Yegar, "Islam and Islamic Institutions in British Malaya, 1974-1941: Policies and Implementation" (Ph.D Thesis, Hebrew University, Jerusalem, 1976); James Low, *The British Settlement at Penang* (Singapore: Oxford University Press, 1972), 273. See also, Hugh Clifford, *Studies in Brown Humanity Being Scrawls and Smudges in Sepia, White and Yellow* (London: Grant Richards, 1898), 229.

[3] Husin Mutalib, *Islam and Ethnicity in Malay Politics* (Singapore: 1990), 23-24. See also Suhaimi Said, *Orang Melayu di Sisi Perlembagaan* (Temerloh: Penerbitan Ujud, 1987), 58.

[4] Merdeka, 50 years of Islamic State?, http://www.jeffooi.com/2007/07/merdeka_50_years_of_islamic_st.php.

[5] Hamid Jusoh, *The Position of Law in the Malaysian Constitution* (Kuala Lumpur: 1991), 31-32.

[6] Mahfuh Halimi, "Islamists Publication in Malaysia," *Global Pathfinder* (Singapore: ICPVTR Database, 16 December 2008).

Mecca in 1979, the continuing Arab-Israel conflict, and the increasing influence of the Middle East given its rich supply of oil.[7]

Around the same time, many radical clerics, including the entire leadership of Darul Islam, the precursor to al-Jama'a al-Islamiyya, received permanent resident status in Malaysia. They managed to influence a few hundred Malaysian youths who became obsessed with jihad as the ultimate embodiment of Islam and rejected democracy and elected representation.[8]

Other Malaysian Islamist movements, particularly those linked to higher learning institutions, began to emerge in the 1980s and 1990s. The Association of Southeast Asian Muslim Students, Indonesian Student Union, and the Islamic International Federation of Student Organization became platforms for the struggle for Muslim rights both nationally and internationally.[9] The movements were inspired by Middle Eastern and South Asian parties and ideologues, most notably the *Ikhwanul Muslimin* (Muslim Brotherhood) founded by Hassan al-Banna (1906-1949) in Egypt, and *Jamaat Islami* (Islamic Group) founded by Syed Abul A'ala Maududi (1903-1979) in India. Like the Middle Easterners that went to study in the West, many Malaysians that went to study overseas returned with ideas that then proliferated into the domestic scene. The influence of these former students is partly due to their social mobility, and also because, as an educated class, they possessed the ability to articulate those ideas convincingly to the wider public. Judith Nagata elegantly describes this educated class as "the Malay students who leave their home shores in Western dress [and] return from the West in Arab garb, with many new ideas underneath."[10]

The proliferation of Islamist books in the market cannot be directly linked to returning students. There is every reason to believe, however, that their continuous discourses in the local media and the subsequent exposure to works of prominent international Islamist ideologues in intellectual gatherings increased the hunger for such publications. The demand for such books in Malaysia resulted in the publication of some leading books in the Islamist genre

---

[7] See Husin Mutalib, "Islamic Revivalism in Asean States," *Asian Survey* 30, no. 9 (September 1990), 877. See also, Mohamad Abu Baker, "External Influences on Contemporray Islamic Resurgence in Malaysia," *Contemporary Southeast Asia* 13 (September 1991), 221-27; Chandra Muzaffar, *Islamic Resurgence in Malaysia* (Petaling Jaya: Penerbit fajar Bakti, 1987).

[8] Jasbir Singh, "Another 10 KMM members arrested: Total arrested now stands at 23 out of a 200-strong group," *New Straits Times*, 25 January 2002.

[9] Mohd Shuhaimi al-Maniri, *Politik Kampus di Sebalik Tabir* (Bandar Baru Bangi: Pustaka generasi Baru, 1995), 118-119.

[10] Judith Nagata, *The Reflowering of Malaysian Islam, Modern Religious Radicals and Their Roots* (Vancouver; University of British Columbia Press, 1984), 58.

at the time. Most of the books focused on issues that were of concern to Islamists around the world, as well as Muslim activists in Malaysia; some of the most influential texts include:

(1) *Gerakan Islam Kini* (Islamic Movement Now) by Fadlullah Clive Wilmot, which was published by Yayasan Dakwah Islamiah Malaysia in 1978. This work explores the rise of the call to return to Islam and make it the basis of Muslim activities, using the Muslim Brotherhood in Egypt and the Islamic Group in India as its examples.[11] Both movements were admired for their holistic and detailed view of Islam and were heralded for having proven the emptiness of systems other than Islam. Overall, the book offers Islam as the solution that can prevent mankind from destruction.

(2) A translation of Maududi's work by Sabri Ahmad with the title, *Pra-syarat Kejayaan Harakah Islamiyyah* (Prerequisite of Success for Islamic Activism), published by Dewan Pustaka Fajar in 1985. This piece works on the assumption that there are many Muslims in the world who want to see the establishment of the Islamic system, and tries to understand the reasons that this vision has not come to fruition.[12] Among the book's conclusions is that Muslims lack sufficient determination in their quest for an Islamic system.

(3) A translation of Dr. Yusuf Qardhawi's work, *Islam Ekstrem: Analisis Dan Pemecahannya* (Extreme Islam: An Analysis and Its Solution), which was republished by Thinker's Library in 1985 from an earlier Indonesian version published by Penerbit Mizan. This work is a response to debates and heated discussions on religious extremism following clashes between Muslim youth and authorities that ended in bloodshed.[13] Intended to be an intellectual study based on the true Islamic teachings, this book discusses the causes of religious extremism.

(4) A translation from Arabic into Malay by Ismail bin Mohd Hassan of Syeikh Muhammad El-Ghazali's *Al-Islam wa At-Thaqaat Al-Mua'thalah*, with the given title, *Islam Dan Tenaga-tenaga yang Terbiar* (Islam and the Neglected Energies), which was published by Siri Penerbitan Yayasan Islam Terengganu in 1986. A critique of Muslims' lethargy in the pursuit of excellence, this book questions the Islamic community's stagnation and how it can be overcome. More specifically, the book seeks to provide

---

[11] Halimi.

[12] Ibid.

[13] Ibid.

answers to such questions as: Who should bear responsibility? What is the value of Muslims' spiritual and intellectual inheritance? Will it prove to be an obstacle that Muslims must be rid of or will it be a source of energy that promises a fresh life?

(5) *Punca Dan Penyelesaian Gejala Kafir-Mengkafir* (Cause and Solution to Overcome The Ex-Communication Phenomenon) by Abu Anas, a translation of Qaradawi's in *Minhuda Al-Islam Fatawa Mu'asirah,* which was published by Dewan Pustaka Fajar in 1988. The book challenges radical Islamist groups' use of excommunication of Muslims considered to be "apostate," and urges overzealous Muslim youth to adopt a path of moderation.[14]

(6) Muhammad Tohir and Abu Laila's translation of Muhammad Qutb's *Jahiliyah al-Qarn al-Isyrin* (Twentieth Century's Ignorance) from Arabic into Malay, published by Victory Agencie in 1989. The title of the book is enough to raise eyebrows, as the 20th Century is generally known for its civilization and progress, as opposed to its ignorance.[15] Yet Qutb argues that a civilization founded on the production of material wealth has nothing to do with knowledge. With this understanding, the book attempts to improve human thoughts and actions to bring them closer to the path of God.

(7) *Islam Politik Dan Pemerintahan* (Political Islam and Governance), translated by Md. Akhir Haji Yaacob into Malay from Dr. Abu Al-Maati Abu Al-Futuh's book in Arabic, which was published in 1990 by Penerbitan Hizbi. A comparison of different political systems, this work uses arguments from Muslim history, as well as arguments based on the Qur'an and the Sunnah, to demonstrate the Islamic point of view.[16]

(8) *Gerakan Dakwah*[17] *Dan Orde Islam Di Malaysia: Strategi Masa Depan* (Missionary Movement and Islamic Order in Malaysia: Future Strategy), published by ABIM (Malaysian Islamic Youth Movement) in 1993. This piece is primarily a compilation of a number of working papers presented in the *Seminar Islam dan Perubahan Soial* in conjunction with ABIM's eighteenth *Muktamar* (party assembly), held in November 1989 at the International Islamic University in Kuala Lumpur. Yet the piece is

---

[14] Ibid.

[15] Ibid.

[16] Ibid.

[17] In general application, *dakwah* means mission or propagation. *Dakwah Islamiyyah* can be considered as the mission or propagation of Islam.

organized with a number of specific modifications made to ensure continuity of ideas from one writer to the next, with the overall theme being that *da'wa* movements should be viewed as "partners in nation building."[18]

(9) *Jenis-Jenis Pemerintah Dan Status Hukumnya Menurut Islam* (Types of Government and Ruling of Its Status in Islam), originally written in Arabic by Dr. Umar Abdurrahman – now in U.S. custody for supporting attacks against landmark targets in New York – under the title *Asnaful Hukkam wa Ahkamuhum*, which was published by Pustaka Syuhada in 1998. This book was written in view of the Islamic revival in many parts of the world, but also recognizes that the phenomenon is not without obstacles. In particular, the book highlights the problem of leadership, arguing that stronger leaders are needed to ensure that Islam is practiced and implemented in its totality. Although the Malay publisher of the book acknowledges the circumstances of the original author, Dr. Umar Abdurrahman, the book has no doubt benefitted Muslim activists in Malaysia.[19]

In sum, these works, while trying to keep abreast with local, regional, and global developments in Islam, were published in Malaysia to provide answers to problems faced by Muslims in that country. While not all of the contents of such works were extremist in nature, they all contributed to the radical Islamist community.

The Development of Threat Groups in Malaysia

The politicization and radicalization phase described above was followed by the formation of threatening groups within Malaysia, and an upswing in support for foreign groups.

Domestic Threat Groups

The primary operational threat from within Malaysia comes from the Kumpulan Militan Malaysia, established in 1995. KMM is described as a satellite of al-Jama'a al-Islamiyya, and its membership also overlaps with that of Malaysia's main opposition party, PAS. The goal of KMM is to overthrow the Malaysian government and establish an Islamic state and thereafter a Southeast Asian Islamic caliphate. The group was founded by Zainon Ismail, a Malaysian from Kedah who fought against the Soviet invasion of Afghanistan. He was succeeded

---

[18] Halimi.

[19] Ibid.

in 1999 by the son of the leader of PAS, Nik Adli Nik Abdul Aziz, who led the group until he was arrested in 2001. Both Nik and his successor, Zulkifli, also fought in Afghanistan against the Soviets. Zulkifli attended primary school in Muar before continuing with his secondary education at Sekolah Datuk Abdul Razak in Seremban from 1979 to 1983, and studied engineering in the United States on a Malaysian government scholarship. Zulkifli fought in Afghanistan for three years, during which time he gained expertise in explosives. He then returned to Malaysia, where he married and had four children.

KMM first came to the attention of the Malaysian authorities after the group attempted to rob the Southern Bank in Petaling Jaya with the intention of raising funds. Twenty-three persons were detained in connection with the attended crime, sixteen of whom were Malaysian. Of these, the majority had studied locally as opposed to overseas.[20] Subsequent arrests of alleged KMM members revealed that several members of the group had received training overseas, particularly in Afghanistan and at two different camps located in the Philippines that belong to JI and the Moro Islamic Liberation Front (MILF). Training also occurred within Malaysia, particularly in the jungles and beaches of Selangor and Johor. This training included mountain climbing and espionage aimed at improving physical and mental fitness.

In addition to bombings of churches and Hindu temples, robberies, and the murder of Lunas assemblyman Dr Joe Fernandez, KMM is alleged to have planned to kill U.S. sailors in Malaysia and to have worked with JI to gather four tons of ammonium nitrate for use against targets in Singapore.

Foreign Threat Groups

    1. Al-Jama'a al-Islamiyya

As evidenced by its connections with KMM, al-Jama'a al-Islamiyya has had a significant influence on the Islamist milieu in Malaysia. JI's origins can be traced back to 1948, when Sekarmadji Maridjan Kartosuwirjo announced the establishment of the Islamic Army of Indonesia (Tentera Islam Indonesia) to fight the newly formed Indonesian republic. Before the Second World War, Kartosuwirjo was active in Muslim nationalist politics in the then Dutch East Indies. He felt unhappy with the pre-independence political maneuvering of the Islamic Masyumi Party's components, and in 1947 began gathering his militia members together in West Java to oppose the secular nature of the Sukarno regime. Darul Islam, established in 1949, actually engaged in hostilities.

---

[20] Singh.

Although Kartosuwirjo was arrested in 1962 and his rebellion crushed that same year, DI had successfully politicized and radicalized many Indonesian Muslims. During Suharto's years in power, beginning in 1966, General Ali Moertopo reactivated DI to protect Indonesia against the danger of communist infiltration across the Indonesian-Malaysian border in Borneo.

In 1977, the Indonesian government arrested some 185 Islamists who were not formally members of DI, but who shared Kartosuwirjo's ideals. The future founders of al-Jama'a al-Islamiyya, Abdullah Sungkar and Abu Bakar Ba'asyir, were among those arrested. Both were deeply involved in *da'wa* activities, were known for making statements urging disobedience to secular authority, and refused to acknowledge the validity of the Indonesian constitution. Sungkar and Ba'asyir were tried in 1982 on charges of being members of DI and sentenced to nine years in prison for subversion. Subsequently their sentences were reduced on appeal to three years and ten months. Facing imminent re-arrest upon their release, they fled to neighboring Malaysia. A charismatic leader, Sungkar emerged as Suharto's number one enemy.

In Malaysia, Sungkar identified a number of sympathetic businessmen willing to take on Indonesian workers and support the establishment of an Islamic state in Indonesia. During the time they were sheltered by Malaysians, the two men continued their teaching and preaching activities, and were ultimately able to have a profound influence on select Malaysian youth.[21] Nasir Abas, a Malaysian who joined DI and subsequently became one of the four regional leaders of JI, later described his own experience as follows:

> In the beginning of 1985, after studying for three months in *Maahad Ittiba'us Sunnah*, there were about 50 Indonesian that came to Malaysia… They seemed so friendly and liked to discuss about Islamic matters. In fact, some of them even brought books to be sold. Almost all books concerned about the Islamic movements such as books written by Hasan al-Banna from *Ikhwanul Muslimin* movement, books concerning the struggle of Afghanistan Mujahidin and Islamic Jihad, others concerning the Islamic belief (*aqidah*) and unity of God (*tauhid*) and the *fiqih* (worship guidance) of prayers. I often bought and borrowed some books from those

---

[21] Bina Bektiati and L. N. Idayanie, "Abu Bakar Who? The Teacher Is Still Here," *TEMPO* (15–21 January 2002).

Indonesian friends some of who I called *Ustaz* [teacher].[22]

In an effort to seek additional funding for their cause, Sungkar and Ba'asyir went to Saudi Arabia, Pakistan, and possibly Afghanistan. This opened the gateway for DI members to gain further military training and exposure to armed jihad. After a dispute with the Indonesian-based DI leader, Ajengan Masduki, Sungkar formed JI in Malaysia on 1 January 1993. By 1995, Sungkar's followers had formed numerous cells consisting of eight-to-ten members who met on a weekly basis to study the Qur'an and prepare for jihad.[23] JI was a more tightly structured organization than DI, but had the same aim of establishing an Islamic state in Indonesia through jihad. Only after JI came into contact with al-Qa'ida did its ambition grow to aspire to a pan-Islamic state in Southeast Asia.

To train the next generation of jihadists, JI established its own schools in Malaysia, including Madrasah Luqmanul Hakiem in Kelantan and in Ulu Tiram, Johor. In addition to physical training, JI dispatched its members to training camps run by al-Qa'ida, most notably Al Farouq, as well as JI camps in Afghanistan and the Philippines, and MILF camps in the Philippines. JI also established a cell in Karachi, the al Ghuraba cell, to train the brothers and sons of JI leaders and members. Hambali, the JI operational leader facilitated regional cooperation through the founding of Rabitatul Mujahidin, a platform through which Southeast Asian jihadist groups could collaborate.

Claiming to be an Islamic revival movement, JI prepared a code of conduct to guide its members. A secret text, the General Guide for Al-Jamaah Al-Islamiyah Struggle (Pedoman Umum Perjuangan Al-Jamaah Al-Islamiyah, or PUPJI), was never published but was made available to the leaders to train the members. In the introduction, the Central Leadership Council of JI wrote that God has outlined a set of principles for mankind to lead their lives. First, the aim of man's creation is to worship Allah alone. Consequently all worldly possessions, time, energy, and thought must be channeled towards this end. Second, the full purpose of human existence on earth is to serve as God's vice-gerent. In this respect, man is responsible for ensuring that the earth is managed and developed within the confine of God's laws. He thus is required to prevent, eliminate, and fight all acts of corruption on earth as a result of the implementation of a way of life that falls outside the domain of God's law. Third, life on earth is a test to filter and sieve members of the human race in order to determine who has performed

---

[22] Nasir Abas, *Membongkar Jamaah Islamiyah: Pengakuan Mantan Anggota JI (Unveiling Jamaah Islamiyah: Confessions of an Ex- JI Member)* (Jakarta: Grafindo Khazanah Ilmu, 2005, English translation), 18-19, 28.

[23] Members of his first small cell included Riduan Isamuddin (alias Hambal)i, Abdul Ghani, Jamsari, Suhauime, Matsah, Adnan, and Faiz Bafana.

the best deed. Good deeds are judged based on the fulfillment of two fundamental requirements, namely sincerity towards God and emulating the Prophet in life's endeavor. Fourth, the apostles of God were sent by Him to establish the *dien*, meaning a way of life based on the unity of God (*Tauhid*), which relates to establishing Islam in all its aspects, as explained by the companion of the Prophet Muhammad, 'Abdullah bin 'Umar, in his commentary of the *Surah Al-Fatehah*, which according to him include '*aqidah* (Islamic creed), '*ibadah* (act of worship), and *manhajul-hayah* (way of life). Like the followers of al-Qa'ida, JI followers believe that the fall of the Ottoman Caliphate in 1924 marked the beginning of an era where the Muslim community became exposed to moral decadence caused by modernity and a secular system. In order to correct this, JI strives to re-establish the Islamic caliphate, selecting Southeast Asia as the place where this vision should be realized.

After Suharto's fall in 1998, JI headquarters shifted from Malaysia to Indonesia.[24] Still, JI Malaysia remained intact, and the Malaysian group continued to control and support JI Singapore. Moreover, Malaysia was used as a launching pad for an attack against two-dozen Indonesian churches on Christmas day in 2000, and as the planning site for contemplated attacks against diplomatic and other targets in Singapore in late 2001/early 2002. Finally, JI continued to influence Muslims across the region with the founding of the Majelis Mujahidin Indonesia (Council of Indonesian Mujahidin, or MMI) in Yogyakarta. An alliance of Islamic groups, MMI advocates the implementation of the *Shari'ah* law. The first Congress, held in Yogyakarta in August 2000, was attended by about fifteen hundred Muslims from all over Indonesia, and ulema (Islamic scholars) from Saudi Arabia, the southern Philippines, and even Malaysia.

Notably, Malaysian authorities long knew of the existence of Indonesian Muslim leaders who opposed Suharto on Malaysian soil. Yet because JI advocated a policy of not attacking any Malaysian targets (out of both expediency and greater tolerance for Islamic government positions), the group was permitted to operate relatively freely until late 2001.[25]

---

[24] Tim Behrend, "Preaching Fundamentalism: The Public Teachings of Abu Bakar Ba'asyir," *Inside Indonesia* (April–June 2003).

[25] The former JI operational leader Hambali went to the extent of stating that there was an understanding between Sungkar and the Malaysian government that JI would not mount any attacks in Malaysia. Although this is unlikely to be true, it is very likely that JI understood the importance of not earning the wrath of the Malaysian authorities. Hambali's debriefing by the US, Guantanamo Bay 2008. According to Nasir Abas, a Malaysian JI member, when Abu Bakar Ba'asyir visited the DI camp in Torkham on the Pakistan-Afghanistan border in 1992, he

2. Al-Qa'ida

Although JI is clearly the dominant foreign threat group operating in Malaysia, prior to 11 September 2001, Malaysia was the central location for al-Qa'ida leaders and operatives to meet, study, invest, and receive medical treatment.[26] For instance, Tawfiq bin Attash (a.k.a., Khallad), the administrator of al-Qa'ida operations, including the 9/11 attack, received his prosthetic leg in Malaysia. Malaysia was also the venue where al-Qa'ida held its last 9/11 planning meeting. In January 2000, the first two hijackers to enter the U.S., Khalid al Midhar and Nawaf al Hamzi, met in the apartment of Yazid Sufaat, a Malaysian microbiologist who headed al-Qa'ida's second anthrax program.[27] That same year, California State University, Sacramento-educated biochemist and retired Malaysian army captain, Sufaat, provided U.S. $35,000 to Zacarias Moussaoui, a French national of Moroccan descent convicted of conspiring to take part in the 9/11 attack.[28] Before relocating to the U.S., Moussaoui unsuccessfully tried to learn to fly wide-bodied aircraft in Malaysia. He also worked with members of al-Qa'ida and JI in Malaysia, assisting them in the procurement of ammonium nitrate to bomb diplomatic and other targets in Singapore. In addition to seeking to influence the Malaysian arena through KMM and JI, al-Qa'ida also invested in establishing a web presence in Malaysia. In fact, al-Qa'ida's first website – alNida.com – was registered in Malaysia.[29]

The Present Landscape of Islamic Extremism in Malaysia

Post-9/11 Crackdown on Operational Threat

Prior to 11 September 2001, Islamic extremists operated relatively freely in Malaysia. This may have been a result of the negative backlash created by the so-called Memali Massacre, an incident occurring in November 1985 in which approximately two hundred Malaysian policemen, operating under orders from the Acting Prime Minister and Home Minister, Musa Hitam, laid siege to a remote village in the Malaysian state of Kedah. The houses were occupied by an Islamic sect of about four hundred people led by Ibrahim Mahmud (a.k.a., Ibrahim Libya), a local religious leader wanted by Malaysian authorities. The

---

explained that Indonesia was the place of first priority to fight for the independence, not Malaysia or Singapore. Nasir Abas, 79.

[26] The National Commission on Terrorist Attacks Upon the United States, *9/11 Commission Report* (Washington D.C.: 22 July 2004), 148, 149, 150, http://www.9-11commission.gov/.

[27] Marc Erikson, "The Osama bin Laden and al-Qaeda of Southeast Asia," *Asia Times*, 6 February 2002.

[28] Ibid.

[29] D. Ian Hopper, "Man Hijacks al-QaidaWeb Site," *Associated Press*, 30 July 2002.

ensuing clash left fourteen civilians and four policeman dead, and led to the arrest of 159 people, including women and children. The incident, which has been chronicled in at least three books published in Malaysia, represents a constant and a continuing source of inspiration and incitement for terrorists and extremists.[30]

The next major crackdown by Malaysian authorities did not come until the June 2001 arrests of KMM members following the group's attempted robbery of a bank in Petaling Jaya, discussed above. Following the 11 September 2001 attacks on the U.S., however, the authorities' net widened to include JI and al-Qa'ida. Indeed, directly following the 9/11 attack, Malaysia's Special Branch (MSB), one of the most respected security and intelligence services in the region, joined forces with Singapore's Internal Security Department (ISD) for the purpose of locating and detaining radical Islamists operating within Malaysia. By December 2001, the security forces had successfully arrested approximately one hundred JI members; however, another three-to-four thousand are believed to have escaped, either by going into hiding or fleeing to Indonesia and Thailand. MSB continues to conduct surveillance and, when necessary, as well as detain foreign and domestic terrorists and terrorist supporters. Additionally, MSB has worked with its overseas counterparts to detect, disrupt, and dismantle a number of cells. Security forces watch religious, political, social, and other community organizations infiltrated by terrorist and extremist groups. Despite the added pressure on radical groups, however, the JI terrorist network remains active and continues to pose a significant threat to the region. Particularly due to its training, financial, and operational links to al-Qa'ida, JI remains able to influence a number of related organizations.[31] At the same time, despite the disagreements between leaders and the formation of new groups, JI ideology continues to grow in influence.[32]

Present Ideological Milieu

---

[30] The first of the three books is *Perisai Memali* (The Memali Shield), by C.N. al-Afghani, which has been banned by the Malaysian government. The second, *Kebangkitan Umat Islam Nusantara Talangsari Warisan Memali* (Uprising of the Muslim Ummah of Nusantara Talangsari Memali's Inheritance), is unofficially circulated in Malaysia. The third book, *Kebangkitan Umat Islam Nusantara Talangsari Warisan Memaliis*, which was published by Penerbitan Pemuda in 1989, compares the Memali Massacre to the Indonesian government's killing of approximately one hundre Muslims in Lampung, South Sumatra, on 7 February 1989.

[31] For instance, influenced by JI, DI leader of West Java Rois recruited DI member Heri Golun as a suicide bomber to attack the Australian High Commission in Jakarta in 2004.

[32] Fatima Astuti, "Islamic Radicalism in Indonesia: The Role of the Asatizahs," *ICPVTR Analysis, Restricted*, 18 November 2008. After resigning from MMI in July 2008, Ba'asyir formed *Jamaah Ansharut Tauhid* (Defender of the Oneness of God JAT) in September 2008.

In addition to the crackdown on the operational threat, the Malaysian government has taken steps since 9/11 to counter the rise of ideological extremism. Most prominently, the former Prime Minister Datuk Seri Abdullah Ahmad Badawi, who was in office from October 2003 until April 2009, reintroduced Islam Hadhari (civilizational Islam), an ideology first put forward by Prime Minister Tunku in 1957. <u>Islam Hadhari</u>, as advocated by the Malaysian government, is based on a set of principles that includes, among others, advancing knowledge in society. The ten principles of Islam Hadhari are: (1) faith and piety in Allah, (2) a just and trustworthy government, (3) a free and independent people, (4) mastery of knowledge, (5) balanced and comprehensive economic development, (6) a good quality of life, (7) protection of the rights of minority groups and women, (8) cultural and moral integrity, (9) safeguarding the environment, and (10) a strong defense policy.[33] Enlightened Malaysian leaders understand this essential balance between traditional Islamic values and modern governmental practices, as well as the need to counter attempts to propagate a culture of extremism. To help prevent the misuse of Islam and its symbols, Badawi, an Islamic scholar himself, remarked: "We want Islam Hadhari to be a tool for Muslims around the world to spread the message that Islam can be a progressive religion without losing its universal values."[34]

Nonetheless, an extremist community influenced by regional and global events subsists in Malaysia. As was the case in the 1980s and 1990s, the extremist milieu in Malaysia is largely nurtured by events taking place beyond the nation's border. Malaysians perceive the Buddhist majority state of Thailand and the Christian majority state of the Philippines to be suppressing the minority Muslim communities fighting for Pattani and Moro independence, respectively. Despite this anger, only a small percentage of Muslims in Malaysia sympathize with terrorist activity. Of that percentage, a tiny minority is politicized, radicalized, and mobilized to provide support for or actively participate in violence. This minority has, so far, included a few dozen members of KMM who traveled to Ambon in eastern Indonesia to fight on the side of Muslims in clashes with Christians that ended in five thousand deaths; Dr Azahari Husin, who was, until his death, the number one bombmaker for JI in Indonesia; and Noordin Mohomed Top, the most wanted JI leader in Indonesia. Generally, Malaysians are inclined to provide support by funding extremists groups and providing safe haven to their operatives.

The Malaysian psyche is also influenced by images and stories from outside of Southeast Asia –Palestine, Lebanon, Chechnya, Afghanistan, and Iraq, as well as other conflict zones. Furthermore, pronouncements by Malaysian leaders blaming the West for injustice, selective media reports highlighting the suffering of the Muslims worldwide, and the Abu Ghraib and Guantanamo Bay abuses

---

[33] "Malaysia Promotes Islam Hadhari," *IslamOnline.net & News Agencies*, 16 March 2007.
[34] Ibid.

have created a wave of anti-Americanism and anti-Zionism among the Malaysians. These feelings are unfortunately reinforced by government policy that supports anti-western institutions and ideas. For instance, while Israeli nationals are denied entry to Malaysia, the country has welcomed Lebanese Hizbollah and Palestinian Hamas leaders and even permitted meetings in Malaysia. Indeed, one of the most popular books in Malaysia is Khaled Hrous's "Hamas: A Beginner's Guide" published by the Islamic Book Trust in 2008.[35] Even the most educated Malaysian leaders, including those who have served at the United Nations, do not regard suicide attacks by Palestinian, Lebanese, Chechen, and Kashmiri groups as acts of "terrorism." At the same time, the highly respected former Prime Minister Mahathir bin Mohomed told the leaders of fifty-seven nations in 2003 that Jews "rule the world by proxy" and "get others to fight and die for them."[36] He called for a "final victory" by the world's 1.3 billion Muslims, who, he said, "cannot be defeated by a few million Jews."[37] Malaysia also hosts many groups allegedly supporting suffering Muslims in conflict zones. Although they take the face of humanitarian groups, several of these organizations—which maintain websites, disseminate propaganda, and raise funds—are either established by or linked to insurgent and terrorist groups.

Against this backdrop, the internet is flourishing as a source for Malaysians to express their frustrations, but also serves to expose them to radical Islamist views. This trend is particularly evidenced by the frequent posting of Malay-language material on such websites as http://abubakr1400.blogspot.com and http://al-tawbah.com. The first of these sites, abubakr1400.blogspot.com, highlights news about persons regarded as holy warriors. For instance, a recent post focused on the Malaysian JI member Yazid, who was recently released from detention.[38] Other examples of material posted since 2006 include:

---

[35] This 192-page book is sold at RM 25. The book blurb states: "The United States calls Hamas a terrorist organisation. Yet Hamas swept to victory in the 2006 Palestinian elections. Why did Hamas win? This one-stop guide to Hamas tells you everything you need to know. The author, a leading Al-Jazeera journalist and Cambridge-based scholar, analyses Hamas's history and its agenda. This book covers all the key issues, including Hamas's attitudes to Israel and the PLO, religious beliefs, suicide bombings and its programme of grassroots social work within Palestine. The reality of Hamas's victory means that the West will now have to engage with it more seriously if there is to be peace in the Middle East."

[36] Prime Minister Mahathir Mohamad of Malaysia, *Address to the Assembly of the Organization of the Islamic Conference*, Putrajaya, Malaysia, 16 October 2003.

[37] Ibid.

[38] This particular posting consisted of material from the New Straits Times. Several other posts on the conditions of the holy warrior have been gathered from other secular media sources, such as Bernama, Al Jazeera, and the Sydney Morning Herald.

- Transcriptions of audio speeches by Ayman Alzawahiri in Malay. This includes one criticizing the Americans for electing Bush for two consecutive terms.

- An audio lecture by Abu Ibrahim entitled *The purpose of Shari'ah.*

- Extremist articles from Indonesian jihadist websites, which include statements and speeches by Abu Bakar Baasyir, the three Bali bombers, and top al-Qa'ida leaders.

- Details of a book authored by Abd Allah ibn Abd al-Bari al-Andal, entitled *The Slicing Sword Against The One Who Forms Allegiances With The Disbelievers And Takes Them As Supporters Instead Of Allah, His Messenger And The Believers.* The topics addressed in the book are: "Muslims emigrating to the lands which were seized by the enemy in order to build up its economy while it remains in their control;" "The Muslim who claims to be from the community of the Christians and identifies himself with their flags, etc.;" "The ruling upon the Muslim who attributes justice to the Christians and approves of their authority and scoffs at the Muslim authority and their leadership;" "The ruling upon the Muslim who ships goods and supplies to the Christian lands and the ruling upon another Muslim who kills him for doing that;" "The ruling upon the Muslims who remain inside the country, which was seized and occupied by foreign invaders, and subsequently fall under their rule;" "The rulings upon those who emigrate to the Muslim lands vs. those who emigrate to the lands of the disbelievers and the effect upon the wealth of both types of emigration;" "The funeral prayer of the one who claims to be from the community of the Christians vs. the funeral prayer for the one who claims to belong to the community of the Muslim Kingdom;" and "The ruling upon the one who turns away from the ruling of Islam in favour of the ruling of the Christian laws."

The second forum frequented by Malay speakers, al-Tawbah.com, focuses heavily on updates of global jihad and news on the mujahidin. Again, statements and speeches from the three Bali bombers and al-Qa'ida leaders are often posted to this site. There are also online conversations between Malay speakers posted on this forum, including a recent thread entitled "Discussion on whether jihad should be fought in one's own country or in other countries." In that thread, one participant, who calls himself "Abu Anshor," submits his view that Patani (a region in Southern Thailand) should be the new focal point of jihad in Southeast Asia. He then goes on to argue that one should not limit oneself to waging jihad in one's own country. Labeling this as a "nationalist" act, Abu Anshor states that he would prefer to have jihad waged in unity with the al-Qa'ida and the Taliban in places like Afghanistan, Chechnya, Iraq, and Somalia. In response, a visitor to the forum writing under the name "Muhibul Terroris" begins by saying that Moro (the Philippines) would be a more legitimate center of jihad in Southeast Asia. He goes on to strongly disagree with Abu Anshor's use of the label "nationalist" for those waging jihad in their home countries, pointing to acts such as the Bali bombings, which he says were committed in the spirit of jihad, not nationalism.

Another worrying trend is that recruitment by Islamic extremists seems to be reaching a much more diverse pool in Malaysia. In the past, most Malaysians who joined JI were from JI-affiliated schools in Malaysia, whereas today, most JI Malaysia members are from secular schools. An instructive example is Mohomed Fadly, born in Jalan Merlimau-Jasin, Melaka in 1985. A student of industrial engineering at Univeristi Teknologi Malaysia, in Skudai, Johore, Fadly received a Public Service Department government scholarship.[39] In June 2007, he was introduced to Ustaz Mohamad, a JI leader wearing a kopiah (a cap) either from Selangor or Johor Bahru, who invited Fadly and several other students to attend classes at an apartment near the university campus.[40] In Ustaz Mohamad's class, Fadly was introduced to classic JI concepts such as the need for Muslims to create a Daulah Islamiah (Islamic state) and the need to perform jihad to elevate the word of God (jihad untuk tinggikan kalimatullah).[41] Indoctrinated into this way of thinking, Fadly began to advocate a classic JI concept, al-wala wal bara (love and hate), where loyalty (wala') is to the Believers (orang-orang beriman), and his enemies (bara') are the infidels (orang-orang kafir), hypocrites (munafiq), and concealed enemies (musuh dalam lipatan).[42] Like other JI members, Fadly took the oath of allegiance (bai'ah) from Ustaz Mohamad in mid-2008.[43] He was asked to intervene in places of crisis (campur tangan dalam tempat-tempat ada krisis) and given a book entitled *Kaedah dan Undang-Undang Jihad* (Methods & Laws of Jihad).[44]

Fadly went through training at Puchong Perdana and Gombak, near International Islamic University Malaysia in Selangor.[45] The training, which lasted for one month, consisted of increasing stamina through push-ups, sit-ups, and leg strengthening exercises.[46] Fadly sometimes questioned his religious training, because the lessons seemed to concentrate only on fighting, and he felt

---

[39] Mohomed Fadly, Member, JI Malaysia, Narathiwat Provincial Prison, 23 March 2009.
[40] Ibid.
[41] Ibid.
[42] Ibid.
[43] Ibid.
[44] Ibid.
[45] Ibid.
[46] Ibid.

that his teachers had a cut-and-paste approach to Islam; however, he felt that raising questions would be useless, and he decided to continue on with his mission.[47] In late 2008, he went with another man to Golok, Thailand to fight on behalf of Muslims.[48] Upon his arrival, Fadly was detained by authorities and imprisoned in Narathiwat prison.[49] Fadly has since stated that he believes Ustaz Mohamed has some ten cells like the one that Fadly joined in Malaysia that may also be recruiting from the general populace.[50]

Looking Forward

The predominant danger that Malaysia faces is the revival of JI and KMM, as well as the rise of extremist groups like Hizbut Tahrir. As terrorism is a by-product of extremism, caution is paramount and constant vigilance is required. As in the past, Malaysia will be used as an area from which terrorist groups plan and coordinate attacks, as well as a point of transit for the transportation of weapons, terrorist operatives, and their supporters to other Southeast Asian nations. Malaysia's vast territorial footprint, centrality in Southeast Asia, and porous coastline generates the potential for Malaysia to be used again as a terrorist safe haven or transit point in the future is very real.

Importantly, the threat of terrorism to Malaysia differs between the various regions. This disparity can be in part attributed to the distinction between eastern and western geopolitics and the differing emphasis that has been undertaken in countering terrorism in each region. In the west, the main threat has come from JI and the KMM, both of which have been dismantled for the time being. In the east, the danger stems from Sabah, the area close to the Sulu Archipelago, "and a porous tri-border sea area between the Philippines, Malaysia and Indonesia."[51] The high potential for terrorist attacks within this area is a result of "decades of poor governance, economic and political marginalization, lack of state capacity, and separatist conflict [which have] turned this area into an 'ungoverned space' and hence a haven for transnational criminals, including terrorists."[52] If not addressed, this black hole near east Malaysia poses a grave problem not only to

---

[47] Ibid.

[48] Ibid.

[49] Ibid.

[50] Ibid.

[51] Ian Storey, "The Triborder Sea Area: Maritime Southeast Asia's Ungoverned Space," *Global Terrorism Analysis* 5, no. 19 (11 October 2007), http://www.jamestown.org/terrorism/news/article.php?articleid=2373708 (last accessed: 27 November 2007).

[52] Ibid.

Malaysia, but also to the other countries in the region, especially Indonesia and the Philippines.

Overall, however, it is critical that Malaysia combat the threat stemming from extremist ideologies, the growth of propaganda, and domestic recruiting. As terrorism is closely linked to politics, good governance is central to threat management. To meet the contemporary security challenges, all countries in the region, including Malaysia, need visionary leaders that could adapt to the changing threat. The dynamic and transnational nature of terrorism makes it essential to upgrade or craft new laws; build new institutions, capabilities, and platforms; and renew existing and expand new partnerships in the fight against Islamic extremism.

The historical development of Jihadi Islamist thought in Indonesia

Greg Barton

Introduction

Claims that Indonesia represents "the second front" in the struggle against jihadi terrorism are very much exaggerated; the threats in South Asia, the Horn of Africa, and the Middle East are in fact much more serious than those in Indonesia. Indeed, the character and influence of Islamic thought and social movements in Indonesia have long been misunderstood. Indonesian society is dominated by moderate civil-sphere organizations; supports many of the world's leading progressive Islamic intellectuals, NGOs, and educational institutions; and has firmly embraced secular, liberal democracy.[1] At the same time, however, Indonesia is more "Islamic" than many commentators recognize, and is no less influenced by modernist-cum-Salafi reformism and radical Islamism than any other large Islamic nation. In fact, social surveys report a surprisingly high level of apparent support for radical Islamic positions, and in the past three legislative elections, around 10 percent of voters have chosen to support radical Islamist parties—a higher percentage than in Pakistan.[2] Furthermore, the long history

---

[1] On progressive Islamic thought in Indonesia see Greg Barton, "The Origins of Islamic Liberalism in Indonesia and its Contribution to Democratisation", in *Democracy in Asia* ed. Michelle Schmigelow (New York: St Martins Press, 1997); Greg Barton, "Neo-Modernism: A Vital Synthesis of Traditionalism and Modernism in Indonesian Islam," *Studia Islamika* 2, no. 3 (1995): 1–75; and Greg Barton, "Indonesia's Nurcholish Madjid and Abdurrahman Wahid as Intellectual Ulama: The Meeting of Islamic Traditionalism and Modernism in Neo-Modernist Thought," *Islam and Christian-Muslim Relations 8*, no. 3 (October 1997): 323–50.

[2] On Islamic politics in Indonesia refer to: Greg Barton, "Islam and Politics in the New Indonesia", in *Islam in Asia: Changing Political Realities,* ed. Jason F Issacson and Colin Rubenstein (eds) (New Jersey: Transaction Press, 2001; Greg Barton, "The Prospects for Islam", in *Indonesia Today: Challenges of History,* ed. Grayson Lloyd and Shannon Smith (Singapore: Institute of Southeast Asian Studies, 2001): 244-55; Greg Barton, "Islam, Islamism and Politics in Post-Soeharto Indonesia," in Islam and Politics in Indonesia, ed. Damien Kingsbury (Melbourne: Monash University Press, 2004); Greg Barton, "Islam and Democratic Transition in Indonesia", in *Religious Organizations and Democratization: Case Studies from Contemporary Asia,* ed. Deborah A. Brown and Tun-jen Cheng (New York: M.E. Sharpe, 2006): 221-41; Greg Fealy, 'Islamic Politics: A Rising or Declining Force?' in *Indonesia: the uncertain transition,* ed. Damien Kingsbury and Arief Budiman (Bathurst, NSW: Crawford House Publishing, 2001; Greg Fealy, "Parties and Parliament: Serving Whose Interests?" in *Indonesia Today: Challenges of History,* ed. Grayson Lloyd and Shannon Smith (Singapore: ISEAS, 2001); and Bachtiar Effendy *Islam and the State in Indonesia* (Singapore: ISEAS, 2003): and Greg Barton, 'Indonesia' in Barry Rubin (ed.) *Global Survey of Islamism,* (New York: M.E. Sharpe, Inc. 2009).

behind jihadi groups such as Jemaah Islamiyah means that Indonesia will have to contend with the threat of jihadi terrorism and radical Islamist violence for the foreseeable future. Assessing this threat requires an understanding of the intellectual genealogy of contemporary jihadi groups in Indonesia.[3]

Interestingly, little analysis has been conducted regarding radical Islamist thought in Indonesia, perhaps becasue Indonesia has yet to produce any jihadi Islamist writers of the caliber of its progressive intellectuals. In fact, its contribution to Islamic thought at the reactionary end of the spectrum remains largely unoriginal and derivative of Middle Eastern and South Asian thinkers. In other words, jihadist thought in Indonesia appears to be entirely an import of the product that sits on the margins of Indonesian religious life and finds greatest appeal in minority groups such as Indonesia's ethnic Arab community. Consequently, it has been relatively easy to dismiss jihadi thought and social movements in Indonesia as aberrations that do not represent, or indeed greatly influence, broader society. However, this attitude ensures insufficient attention paid to the unique way in which radical Indonesian Muslims have blended the two competing traditions of Muslim Brotherhood political activism and Saudi Wahhabi Salafism.

This chapter begins by exploring the foundations of this distinctive blend of radical Islamic thought, laid over the last century in the wake of Islamic modernism. It then explores the violent insurgency of the proto-jihadist Darul Islam movement in the 1950s and the growth of political activism in the 1980s and 1990s, which coincided with the spread of the radical ideas tied to the post-Iranian Revolution Middle East, as well as the Salafi zeal fuelled by Saudi funding further amplified by the mujahidin struggle in Afghanistan. Finally, the chapter looks at the current state of radical Islamist thought in Indonesia.

Islamic Modernism and Salafi Thought in Indonesia

Indonesia is unique amongst Muslim-majority nations in that it has two large mass-based Islamic organizations holding sway over the majority of observant Muslims. With a population of around 245 million people, 87 percent of whom identify as Muslims, Indonesia is home to approximately 215 million Muslims. Based on indirect indicators such as voting patterns, educational affiliations,

---

[3] See Robert W. Hefner, *Civil Islam: Muslims and Democratization in Indonesia* (Princeton, NJ: Princeton University Press, 2000): xix; 214-21; and Giora Eliraz, *Islam in Indonesia: Modernism, Radicalism and the Middle East Dimension* (Brighton: Sussex Academic Press, 2004).

Ramadan fast observance, and attendance at Friday prayer, roughly half of these are observant believers, known in Indonesia as *santri* Muslims. *Santri* Muslims are, in turn, largely divided between urban Islamic modernists and rural traditionalists. The vast majority of modernists are affiliated with an organization called Muhammadiyah, which was founded in 1912 as a reformist movement that advocated individual interpretations of the Qur'an over acceptance of traditional interpretations laid down by the *ulama*. The other main modernist organizations include al-Irsyad, founded in 1913, and Persis, founded in the 1923.[4] While these groups have much smaller memberships, they do enjoy a disproportionate influence upon Islamist politics and activism. The majority of the rural Islamic traditionalists, by contrast, are directly linked to an organization called Nahdlatul Ulama (NU), which was established in 1926 in reaction to the establishment of Muhammadiyah.[5]

Muhammadiyah is generally recognized as a moderate organization that has consistently played a constructive role in Indonesia, particularly in the areas of education and health. While it is true that Muhammadiyah is, sociologically, a moderate organization, it has also long been an intellectually conservative organization with strong reactionary elements. In fact, although theoretically based on the ideas of Muhammad Abduh, the Egyptian jurist and religious scholar regarded as the father of Islamic modernism, Muhammadiyah is shaped more directly by the ideas of Abduh's disciple, Rashid Rida. Rida, who inherited the mantle of Muhammad Abduh after the latter's death in 1905, propagated and built upon the ideas of Abduh via his journal, *al-Manar*. After moving from his native Syria to Cairo in 1897, Rida worked closely with Muhammad Abduh.

---

[4] On Persis see: Howard M. Federspiel, *Islam and Ideology in the Emerging Indonesian State: the Persatuan Islam (Persis) 1923-1957* (Leiden: Brill, 2001).

[5] On Islamic Modernism in Indonesia see Islamic modernism in Indonesia and Muhammadiyah see: B.J. Boland, *The Struggle of Islam in Modern Indonesia* (The Hague: Martinus Nijhoff, 1971); Charles Kurzman (ed.), *Modernistl Islam: A Sourcebook* (Oxford: Oxford University Press 2002); Mitsuo Nakamura, *The Crescent Arises over the Banyan Tree: A Study of the Muhammadiyah Movement in a Central Javanese Town* (Yogyakarta: Gadjah Mada University Press, 1983); and Deliar Noer, *The Modernist Muslim Movement in Indonesia* (Kuala Lumpur: Oxford University Press, 1973). On Islamic tradionalism in Indonesia see: Greg Barton and Greg Fealy, eds., *Nahdlatul Ulama, Traditional Islam and Modernity in Indonesia* (Clayton, Australia: Monash Asia Institute, 1996); Greg Barton, *Abdurrahman Wahid, Indonesian President, Muslim Democrat: A View from the Inside* (Sydney and Honolulu: UNSW Press and University of Hawaii Press, 2002); Greg Fealy, "Rowing in a Typhoon: Nahdlatul Ulama and the Decline of Constitutional Democracy", in *Indonesian Democracy: 1950s and 1990s*, ed. David Bourchier and John Legge (Clayton, Australia: Monash University, 1994), 88–98.

Nevertheless, Rida had a very different background from Abduh, and maintained a very different world view. Whereas the latter had spent years living and studying in Europe, where he gained a deep appreciation of Western thought and culture, Rida was deeply skeptical of the West, having experienced only the worst of Europe through its imperialism in the Middle East, not having travelled to Europe or mastered its languages. Hence, the modernist ideas that Rida articulated following the Abduh's death were increasingly dominated by critiques of European imperialism and rejection of European culture; much of Abduh's emphasis on the importance of borrowing that which is best from the West was lost in transmission through Rashid Rida. Instead, in Rida's hands, Islamic modernism gave way to proto-Islamism.

Rida's rejection all aspects of Islamic mysticism is particularly important for understanding the development of Muhammadiyah as an institution focusing on cleansing Islam (i.e. separating "superstitious practices" of traditionalist folk-Islam). As a result, Muhammadiyah focused on modern secular education, excluding of Islamic scholarship, and soon lacked the capacity for any intellectual self-regeneration, blocking its own engagement in *ijtihad*. The members of Muhammadiyah thus had a continual need for religious advice and guidance in the form of *fatwa*, or legal rulings, from external religious experts. In 1927, Muhammadiyah leader K.H. Mas Mansur sought to address this problem by establishing the Perkumpulan Musyawaratul Ulama (The Ulama Consultative Assembly), later renamed the Majelis Tarjih (The Council for Religious Interpretation). Over time, the *fatwa* and determinations produced by the Majelis Tarjih were assembled in serialized collections known as Himpunan Putusan Tarjih (the Compilations of Tarjih Decisions), becoming its own body of law that in time replaced both the classical *mazhab* and any *ijtihad* outside that undertaken by the Majelis Tarjih experts. Muhammadiyah produced very few of its own *ulama* within Indonesia and became dependent upon *ulama* educated in Middle Eastern institutions that were regarded as reformist, rather than traditionalist. With few exceptions, the Majelis Tarjih has been dominated by Wahhabi Salafi thinking.

By the 1930s, the emphasis on Wahhabi Salafism was accompanied by a parallel interest in Islamism. In particular, the combination of Wahhabi Puritanism in religious thinking and anti-colonial nationalism in political thinking led Muhammadiyah leaders to be increasingly attracted to the embryonic Islamist ideas of Hassan al-Banna, the founder of the Muslim Brotherhood in Egypt. When first established in 1928, the Muslim Brotherhood attracted the support of only a few hundred people, but within just ten years, its support base expanded exponentially, quickly claiming over 200,000 members. The success of Al-Banna's movement was driven by an intellectual combination: ideas of Wahhabi Salafism and Abduh's modernism. The political thought carried on by Rashid Rida helped to create a political movement dedicated to restoring the purity of Islamic society and re-establishing the caliphate. In other words, he advocated replacing weak nation-states with a vigorous Islamic empire, appealing to widely to the Muslim world. Abul Ala Maududi—who would later found Jamaat-e-Islami, currently the oldest political party in Pakistan— also heavily influenced Muhammadiyah's leaders around this time, both directly through his writings and indirectly through his influence on Hassan al-Banna's thought. Maududi's early books, which included *Towards Understanding Islam* (1932),*The Problem of Nationalism* (1937), and *Muslims and the Present Political Crisis* (1939), introduced key concepts such as "theo-democracy" and sketched out the cardinal ideas of Islamism.[6]

Darul Islam—Radical Islamism Turns Against the State

In the 1950s, the non-violent civil-sphere activism of groups such as Muhammadiyah was augmented with the guerrilla warfare and violent insurgency of the proto-jihadist Darul Islam (DI) movement. The DI story, we now realize, is considerably more complex than initially acknowledged. It has always been tempting to think of DI as a relatively insignificant aberration and transitory phenomenon of no lasting consequence. Yet the fact that the DI movement eventually gave rise to the network of jihadist Islamists that became Jemaah Islamiyah has forced us to reconsider our understanding of Darul Islam.

Darul Islam is reasonably well known but the back-story behind its founder, Sekarmadji Maridjan Kartosuwirjo, is much less so. Like the first president of independent Indonesia, Sukarno, Kartosuwirjo was raised as a member of the

---

[6] Regarding the development of radical Islamist and Salafi influence in Indonesia refer to: Robert W. Hefner, "Civic Pluralism Denied? The New Media and Jihadi Violence in Indonesia," in *New Media in the Muslim World: The Emerging Public Sphere*, ed. Dale F. Eickelman and Jon W. Anderson (Bloomington: Indiana University Press, 2003), 158–79; Robert W. Hefner "Print Islam: Mass Media and Ideological Rivalries in Indonesian Islam", *Indonesia* 64 (October 1997): 77-103; William R. Liddle, "Media Dakwah Scriptualism: One form of Islamic Political Thought and Action in New Order Indonesia", in *Intellectual Development in Indonesian Islam* ed. Mark Woodward and James Rush (Tempe: Centre for Southeast Asian Studies, Arizona State University, 1996): 71-107; Arskal Salim and Azyumardi Azra (eds.) *Shar'ia and Politics in Modern Indonesia* (Singapore: ISEAS, 2003); Muhammad Sirozi, "The Intellectual Roots of Islamic Radicalism in Indonesia", The Muslim World no. 95 (January 2005): 81-120; and Martin Van Bruinessen, "Genealogies of Islamic Radicalism in Post-Suharto Indonesia", *South East Asia Research* 10, no. 2 (2002): 117–24.

small Dutch-educated elite at the apex of indigenous East Indies society. Both men were drawn towards the charismatic leader of Sarekat Islam (Islamic Trade Union), Haji Oemar Said (H.O.S.) Tjokroaminoto. Founded in 1912 in the city of Solo/Surakarta, later home to Jemaah Islamiyah founders Abdullah Sungkar and Abu Bakar Ba'asyir, Sarekat Islam was, in essence, Indonesia's first political party, although it only formally declared itself as such in 1928.[7] Kartosuwirjo quickly established himself as a protégé of Tjokroaminoto, becoming his private secretary and confidant. Initially, Kartosuwirjo had to compete with Sukarno, four years his senior, for the attention of Tjokroaminoto. Indeed, the handsome, self-confident Sukarno had so impressed his mentor that he was offered his daughter's hand in marriage. Yet Sukarno, a socialist and admirer of Turkey's Mustafa Kemal Ataturk, split with Sarekat Islam in 1927 to form the Indonesian National Party (Partai Nasional Indonesia, or PNI). By contrast, Kartosuwirjo, who grieved for the Ottoman caliphate and bemoaned the secularizing reforms of Ataturk, went on to become the vice president of Sarekat Islam in 1937. By this time, Kartosuwirjo had become well known for promoting the idea of independent Indonesia being an Islamic state.

The birth of the Darul Islam movement may be traced to Kartosuwirjo's formation of a militia in West Java to fight against Dutch colonialism. In January 1948, towards the end of the struggle for independence, Kartosuwirjo learned that Hezbollah, the Islamic-nationalist militia that he had led throughout the revolution, was being squeezed out of post-revolutionary affairs.[8] Unlike the members of many of the other militia who had struggled against the Dutch, his men were not being offered places in TNI, the post-independence Indonesian National Army. Kartosuwirjo thus decided that the time had come for Hezbollah to make a clean break from the secular nationalist forces with which it had an uneasy relationship. On 7 August 1949, as the nationalist victory over the colonial forces was reaching its conclusion, Kartosuwirjo moved to formally

---

[7] Besides Kartosuwirjo and Sukarno, Sarekat Islam launched the nationalist careers of a number of Indonesia's leading figures. This diverse group included Semaun, who became the Communist Party of Indonesia's first chairman in 1921 before the socialists within Sarekat Islam were forced out of the organization. Prominent West Sumatran nationalist leader Haji Agus Salim, one of the nine who drafted the Pancasila, joined in 1915 and went on to draw in future prime minister Mohammad Roem and Persis activist and future Masyumi leader Muhammad Natsir. Despite having a strong socialist wing, Sarekat Islam was also very close to many within the ultra-conservative Persis and these figures exercised a strong influence over Kartosuwirjo.
[8] Note that the name Hezbollah means the faction, or party, of God and is a common name for Islamist militia.

declare the Hezbollah controlled areas of West Java to be the Islamic State of Indonesia (Negara Islam Indonesia, or NII), or Darul Islam.

The second front for the Darul Islam movement came in 1952 when Kahar Muzakkar, the Hezbollah leader in South Sulawesi, linked-up with Kartosuwirjo. Despite the Islamic cast of the Hezbollah militia in South Sulawesi, prior to establishing links with Kartosuwirjo, Muzakkar had not previously shown any great interest in leading a religious movement. The dispute in South Sulawesi with the nationalist forces in Jakarta was born out of regional disaffection rather than Islamist conviction. In fact, in 1945, Muzakkar was a nationalist solider so trusted that he was one of Sukarno's personal bodyguards, and had been sent into the jungles of South Sulawesi to negotiate the surrender of rebel forces. As with the case in West Java, irritation at post-revolutionary roles sparked confrontation. Without this trigger, and the increasing influence of Kartosuwirjo upon Muzakkar, it is unlikely that separatist Islamism would have replaced regional disaffection as the driving ideological force in South Sulawesi.

Finally, there was an often overlooked third front for the Darul Islam movement, which opened up in Aceh under the leadership of Daud Beruah. In fact, Gerakan Aceh Merdeka, which was formed in 1976, drew upon families previously involved with the Aceh Darul Islam movement. Unlike the case with West Java and South Sulawesi, however, radical Islamism did not endure as the dominant ideology in Aceh's separatist cause.

In 1962, Kartosuwirjo was arrested and, although Muzakkar avoided arrest for several more years, he was killed in a 1965 encounter with the TNI. At that point, the Darul Islam movement appeared to have run its course with the passing of its leaders. Such misjudgment only became fully apparent in the wake of the 2002 Bali bombings.

Dewan Dakwah Islamiyah Indonesia (DDII) — Muslim Brotherhood Methods and Wahhabi Salafi Ideas Find a Common Outlet

The next important step in the formation of Indonesian Islamist thought came with the banning of the modernist Islamic party Masyumi in January 1960. The party was banned for alleged support of a dissident movement in West Sumatra, leading many of the senior Masyumi leaders to turn to non-party political activism. Among them was Muhammad Natsir (1907-1993), who led Masyumi through the 1950s. Specifically, Natsir decided to establish a new organization to lead Indonesian Muslims to a deeper commitment to their faith and to reform their understanding of Islam. Natsir's new organization, Dewan Dakwah

Islamiyah Indonesia (DDII), was very much inspired by the ideas of Egypt's Muslim Brotherhood.[9] These were hardly new ideas for Natsir, who had been a member of the Salafist Persis organization. Indeed, although Natsir was seen by many of his colleagues in the 1950s as an innovative and rather progressive figure. He was influenced by the ideas of Maududi and the Muslim Brotherhood, including the ideas of Sayyid Qutb. At the same time, Natsir was very open to Saudi Salafi ideas, prompting him to look to Saudi Arabia for assistance. This led to an alliance between the Saudi-based Muslim World League (Rabita al-Alam al-Islami) and Muhammad Natsir, with the Rabita investing heavily in DDII. The vast majority of Islamist leaders to emerge in Indonesian society over the next forty years benefited from and were shaped by this alliance.

One of the joint projects undertaken by DDII and the Saudi government was the establishment of the Institute for the Study of Arabic (Lembaga Pengetahuan Bahasa Arab—LPBA) in Jakarta, which in 1980 was renamed the Institute for the Study of Islam and Arabic (LIPIA). The institute was established when leading Saudi state cleric Shayk Bin Baz tasked one of his most trusted students, Abdul Aziz Abdullah Al-Ammar, to travel to Jakarta to meet with Muhammad Natsir. He was tasked with establishing LPBA in Jakarta as an overseas branch of the Islamic University Imam Muhammad Ibn Saud in Riyadh. Some of the key early alumni of LIPIA include: Abdul Hakim Abdat, Yazid Jawwas, Farid Okbah, Ainul Harits, Chamzah Sofwan, Abu Bakar M. Altway, Ja'far Umar Thalib, Yusuf Usman Baisa, and Ainur Rafiq Ghufran.

LIPIA alumnus Yusuf Usman Baisa continued his study at the Islamic University Imam Muhammad Ibn Saud in Riyadh, and then returned to Indonesia to establish the al-Irsyad *pesantren* in Salatiga. Another alumnus, Chamzah Sofwan (also known as Abu Nida) also continued his study at the Islamic University Imam Muhammad Ibn Saud in Riyadh and then went on to become a key figure in Indonesia's new Islamism. After graduating from Riyadh in 1985, he spent three months with the Jamaah Da'wah Mujahidin faction led by Jamilul Rahman on the Pakistan–Afghanistan border. Returning to Indonesia from Afghanistan, he initially taught at Pesantren al-Mukmin in Ngruki, the *pesantren* infamously associated with Jemaah Islamiyah, and the finally settled at the DDII-linked Pesantren Ibn al-Qayyim in Yogyakarta. Yet another famous LIPIA graduate is

---

[9] On Dewan Dakwah refer to: Robert W. Hefner, *Civil Islam: Muslims and Democratization in Indonesia* (Princeton, NJ: Princeton University Press, 2000) 167-213; Noorhaidi Hasan, *Laskar Jihad: Islam, Militancy, and the Quest for Identity in Post-New Order Indonesia* (Ithaca: Cornell Southeast Asia Program, 2006).

Ja'far Umar Thalib, erstwhile leader of Laskar Jihad. After graduating from LIPIA, Thalib went to Lahore, Pakistan to study at the Maududi Institute. In 1987, he spent two years with Jamilul Rahman as part of the mujahidin struggle against the Soviet Union in Afghanistan. He then taught for a while at Pesantren Yusuf Baisa before going to Yemen to study under the famous Salafi teacher Syeikh Muqbil ibn Hadi Al-Wadi' in Dammaz. After returning to Indonesia, Jaffar Umar Thalib established Laskar Jihad in Yogyakarta.

In its early days, DDII was seen as reasonably moderate, albeit with a clearly Salafi position. Over the years, however, Dewan Dakwah grew more reactionary. In the 1970s, the Central Java branch of DDII was led by Abdullah Sungkar. Sungkar was one of those in the organization with more extreme views than Natsir, and it was this element responsible for the establishment of the Committee for Solidarity with the Islamic World, or KISDI, in 1987. By that time, it was clear that the long-deferred aspirations of Islamist party-politics held very little appeal to the generations of Indonesian Muslims who had grown up since Masyumi. Lukman Harun, one of the initiators of KISDI, recognized that while young Muslims had little passion for reviving Masyumi, they were passionately concerned about the fate of the Palestinians and other suffering Muslim communities. He decided to develop a vehicle to harness their concern. A decade later, KISDI gave rise to a new group with links to Dewan Dakwah, known as KOMPAK, which was to play an instrumental role in recruiting mujahidin through propoganda videos and literature to defend their brothers in Ambon and Poso.

Meanwhile, the thinking of younger Islamists was being shaped by a plethora of key Islamist texts that first became available in translation in the 1980s. In the four years from 1982 to 1986, twenty-nine seminal radical Islamist works were translated and published in Indonesia. These included three books by Al-Banna, sixteen volumes by Sayyid Qutb, ten books by Maududi, and six books by Iran's Ali Shariati.

Another trend that developed in the 1980s among younger Islamists was campus activism, including Tarbiyyah activism, which is intimately linked with the ideas of the Muslim Brotherhood. These university movements did not emerge directly from either Muhammadiyah or from DDII, but rather had their genesis in student activism associated with the Salman Mosque community on the campus of Indonesia's prestigious Bandung Institute of Technology (ITB). Hizb ut-Tahrir has its origins in the activism of ITB students associated with the Al-Ghifari mosque at the University of Gadjah Mada (UGM) in Yogyakarta, one of

Indonesia's leading universities, and with students involved in the so-called Da'wah Salafi in Yogyakarta that was connected with the Sholehuddin Mosque.

The jihadi Islamists of Da'wah Salafi used mosques such as the Mardiyah Mosque (near UGM) and the Mujahidin Mosque (also in Yogyakarta), *pesantren*, and secular university campuses as their arena for *dakwah* activism. With the financial support of Salafi institutions in Saudi Arabia, Kuwait, and other Gulf countries, they built mosques and extended their *dakwah* networks throughout almost all of Indonesia's major cities. They established periodicals, such as *AsSunah* (in 1994), and publishing houses, such as Pustaka Azzam, Pustaka AsySyafii, and Alkautsar; produced numerous tape cassette and VCD/DVD series, such as *tasjil al-shafwah*; established a multitude of websites and foundations, such as Alshofwah in Degolan Kaliurang, Jamilur Rahman, Assunnah, Majlis Ihya' Turath Al-Islami, Alhuda in Bogor, Nurussunnah in Semarang, Wahdah Islamiyyah in South Sulawesi; and founded several *pesantren*, including Pesantren Wathaniyyah Islamiyyah in Kebumen, Al-Furqon in Gresik, Al-Irsyad in Salatiga, and At-Turath Al-Islami. These new channels of *dakwah*, established in the 1980s and 1990s, laid a foundation for Salafist activism in the period following Suharto's leader's resignation in May 1998.

The Origins of Jemaah Islamiyah

Jemaah Islamiyah co-founder Abdullah Sungkar was born in 1937 in Solo, Central Java into an Indonesian-Hadrami (Yemeni) family.[10] The other co-

---

[10] For studies on Jemaah Islamiyah Jemaah Islamiyah refer to: Zachary Abuza, *Political Islam and Violence in Indonesia* (London: Routledge, 2007); Greg Barton, *Indonesia's Struggle: Jemaah Islamiyah and the Soul of Islam* (Sydney: UNSW Press, 2004); Greg Fealy and Anthony Bubalo, *Between the Global and the Local: Islamism, the Middle East, and Indonesia*, Analysis Paper No. 9, The Brookings Project on U.S. Policy Towards the Islamic World (Washington D.C.: The Saban Center for Middle East Policy at The Brookings Institution, 2005); Greg Fealy and Aldo Borgu, *Local Jihad: Radical Islam and Terrorism in Indonesia*, (Canberra: Australian Strategic Policy Institute, 2005); and Maria Ressa, *Seeds of Terror: An Eyewitness Account of al-Qaeda's Newest Center of Operations in Southeast Asia* (New York: Free Press, 2003). See also the excellent reports from the Jakarta office of the International Crisis Group (ICG) under Sidney Jones, based on first-hand observation, interviews and field research: International Crisis Group Asia Briefing, "Al-Qaeda in Southeast Asia: The Case of the 'Ngruki Network' in Indonesia", August 8, 2002; ICG, "'Deradicalisation' and Indonesian Prisons", *Asia Report* N°142 (19 November 2007); ICG, "Indonesia: Jemaah Islamiyah's Current Status", *Asia Briefing* N°63 (3 May 2007); ICG, "Terrorism in Indonesia: Noordin's Networks", *Asia Report* N°114 (5 May 2006); ICG, "Recycling Militants in Indonesia: Darul Islam and the Australian Embassy Bombing", *Asia Report N°92* (22 February 2005); ICG, "Indonesia Backgrounder: Why Salafism and Terrorism Mostly Don't Mix", *Asia Report* N°83 (13 September 2004); ICG, "Indonesia: Violence Erupts Again in Ambon", *Asia Briefing* N°32 (17 May

founder, Abu Bakar Ba'asyir, whose family was also of Hardrami descent, was born in Jombang, East Java in 1938. As young men in the mid-1950s, Sungkar and Ba'asyir were active in Gerakan Pemuda Islam Indonesia, the Masyumi-linked youth organization. Ba'asyir went on to become involved in the Islamist organization al-Irsyad, which drew most of its members from families with ethnic Arab connections, Hadrami in particular.[11] Like many prominent Islamic leaders in Indonesia—including the late progressive thinker Nurcholish Madjid and the current leader of Muhammadiyah, Din Syamsuddin—Ba'asyir also spent several years studying at the famous Pondok Gontor *pesantren* in East Java.

In 1967, Sungkar and Ba'asyir, by then close friends, took their *dakwah* activism to a broader audience by setting up Radio Dakwah Islamiyah Surakarta in Solo (also known as Surakarta). Then, in 1971, Sungkar and Ba'asyir established Pesantren al-Mu'min in temporary premises in the district of Solo. Four years later, Pesantren al-Mu'min moved to the village of Ngruki on the outskirts of Solo, where it continues to function today, remaining Ba'asyir's home base.

In 1977, the authorities arrested 185 activists linked to Komando Jihad—a group believed to be made up of Darul Islam—including two key leaders: Haji Islamail Pranoto (popularly known as Hispan), who had become close to Sungkar and Ba'asyir, and Haji Danu Mohamad Hasan. Significantly, both men were close associates of Kartosuwirjo, the founder of DI, and both spoke of setting up Islamic *jemaah*, or communities, along the lines of Darul Islam's original vision. The arrests succeeded in flushing out an array of underground Islamist networks that had been brought together under the rubric of Komando Jihad. Once identified and out in the open, the security authorities moved to arrest many of the members of Komand Jihad, including Sungkar and Ba'asyir, who were detained in 1978. Sungkar and Ba'asyir were released in 1982 and subsequently enjoyed several years of active recruiting as they exploited their increased profile and the moral capital gained from having been jailed by the regime.

2004); ICG, "Indonesia Backgrounder: Jihad in Central Sulawesi", *Asia Report* N°74 (3 February 2004); ICG, "Jemaah Islamiyah in South East Asia: Damaged but Still Dangerous", *Asia Report* N°63 (26 August 2003); ICG, "Indonesia Backgrounder: How The Jemaah Islamiyah Terrorist Network Operates", *Asia Report* N°43 (11 December 2002); ICG, "Impact Of The Bali Bombings", *Asia Briefing* N°23, 24 (October 2002); ICG, "Indonesia: Resources and Conflict in Papua", *Asia Report* N°39 (13 September 2002); ICG, "Al-Qaeda in Southeast Asia: The case of the 'Ngruki Network' in Indonesia" (Corrected on 10 January 2003), *Asia Briefing* N°20 (8 August 2002).
[11] On Indonesia's Hadrami community and their political affiliations, including al-Irsyad see: Natalie Mobini-Kesheh, *The Hadrami Awakening: Community and Identity in the Netherlands East Indies 1900-1942* (Ithaca: Cornell Southeast Asian Program, 1993).

Working out of Ngruki, Ba'asyir concentrated on building up small communities by working with even smaller study cells, called *usroh*, which consisted of eight to fifteen members. Members swore an oath of obedience to Ba'asyir (so long as he did not stray from the true path of Islam), were required adherents to separate themselves from all *kafir* institutions, including schools and other agencies of the Indonesian state, and follow a strict Salafi understanding of *sharia* law.[12] Inspired by the remarkable success of the Islamic revolution in Iran several years earlier, and tapping into widespread anger at the Suharto regime's heavy-handed secularization of religious organizations, all of which were required to swear ideological allegiance to Pancasila—the political philosophy of Indonesian state, originally decreed by President Sukarno—radical Islamist groups attracted broad support across Indonesia. This was particularly evident in the university cities of Solo and Yogyakarta in Central Java, where the newly released Sungkar and Ba'asyir were heroes to many.

The Sudirman Mosque in the Sleman district of Yogyakarta, and its associated youth movement known as the Coordinating Body of Mosque Youth (Badan Koordinasi Pemuda Masjid, or BKPM) became a magnet for a number of angry young men who would later join Jemaah Islamiyah. One such young man was Gontor graduate Irfan S. Awwas, who rose to prominence by his fiery reporting of the 1982 trial of Sungkar and Ba'asyir, for which he was to spend a decade in prison on charges of subversion himself. Others included Awwas's brother, Fikiriddin, the current executive chairman of MMI, and later JI activist Agus Dwikarna.[13]

In September 1984, the Indonesian military signaled that it was prepared to use harsh measures to curtail the growth of underground Islamist movements when

---

[12] International Crisis Group, "Al-Qaeda in Southeast Asia: The Case of the 'Ngruki Network' in Indonesia," *Asia Briefing*, 8 August 2002, 10.

[13] International Crisis Group Asia Briefing, "Al-Qaeda in Southeast Asia: The Case of the 'Ngruki Network' in Indonesia", August 8, 2002, 10. Agus Dwikarna came into the Ngruki circle through his friendship with Irfan Awwas, which formed when they were both student activists. Dwikarna personifies a direct link between the Darul Islam movement in Southern Sulawesi and JI. He was the leader of Laskar Jundullah, the armed "security" wing of the Makassar-based Darul Islam successor KPSI (Committee for Upholding Islamic Law, or Komite Pengerak Syariat Islam). The secretary general of KPSI is Abdul Aziz Qahhar Muzakkar, son of Darul Islam leader Kahar Muzakkar.[13] Another significant link came via Muzakkar's son-in-law, Abdul Wahid Kadungga. Kadunnga gave assistance to Sungkar and Ba'asyir when they first moved to Malaysia in the mid-1980s. More importantly, however, he is also believed to have provided a direct link to al-Qa'ida via Gama Islami, the radical break-away wing of Egypt's Muslim Brotherhood.

it made a bloody intervention in Jakarta's port district of Tanjung Priok to break up a protest involving *usroh* activists, killing dozens. Then, on the 21 January 1985, a former Ngruki lecturer bombed the massive 9th century Buddhist Stupa, Borobudur, in Central Java. Shortly afterwards, the Indonesian Supreme Court heard an appeal against Sungkar and Ba'asyir's 1982 release from prison and ruled in the prosecution's favor, issuing summons for the pair. Upon hearing this, Sungkar and Ba'asyir decided to make a *hijrah*, or strategic retreat, to Malaysia.[14] Thus, in April 1985, Sungkar, Ba'asyir, and a small group of followers left for Malaysia, as other Indonesians have done.[15] In the fifteen years that followed, the Malaysian exiles kept close links via couriers with *jemaah* members in Solo and Jakarta, where many BKPM members had moved after the arrest of Irfan Awwas. A small community was also established in a shared house in the district of Pisangan Lama in East Jakarta.

Shortly after settling in Malaysia, Sungkar and Ba'asyir travelled to Saudi Arabia to seek funding for their community. Upon returning to Malaysia, the two organized trips to Afghanistan for Southeast Asian recruits to fight against Soviet occupation. The first small group of mujahidin made the trip in 1985. Thos recruiting for the Afghan campaign hoped that large numbers of fighters would come from Southeast Asia, but Sungkar and Ba'asyir were careful about who they endorsed. The following year's group, however, was as large as fifty or sixty. We now understand that virtually all of the senior leadership of what became Jemaah Islamiyah studied and trained between 1985 and 1995 in camps in the mountainous border region between Afghanistan and Pakistan. There were many other Southeast Asians among the "Afghan alumni," as they came to be known, but only some of them later joined JI. Many of these non-JI alumni nevertheless became trusted associates of JI in groups such as Darul Islam and its related organizations, whether in West Java or South Sulawesi, smaller independent groups, or somewhat more distant organizations such as the Moro Islamic Liberation Front (MILF) or the Abu Sayyaf Group (ASG) in the Philippines. Some of those who became key figures in JI were also formally inducted into al-Qa'ida itself, although this was not a common pattern, as al-Qa'ida was very selective. Thus, friendships formed in Afghanistan/Pakistan often bridged otherwise unconnected groups, such as JI and ASG, or MILF and ASG, and laid the foundations for future collaboration.

---

[14] The word *hijrah* invokes the example of the Prophet Muhammad's retreat to Medina when the people of Mecca turned against him and reject the message of God
[15] Malaysia, a nation of 27 million citizens, is thought to have several million illegal "guest workers"—mostly Indonesian—without valid travel documentation.

The majority of foreign (that is to say, non-Afghan and non-Pakistani) fighters in Afghanistan were ethnic Arabs from heartland Arab states such as Egypt, Saudi Arabia, Jordan, and Syria, but significant numbers of mujahidin also came from northern Africa, Europe, the Caucuses, and Southeast Asia. In March 1985, the war reached its bloodiest phase. In response, Saudi recruiting of foreign fighters intensified and agencies such as the Rabitah stepped up their efforts to recruit and finance foreign fighters. As a result, funding was seldom a problem for Sungkar and Ba'asyir, but they were nevertheless careful about who they sent to Afghanistan. In many ways, those in their first several groups represented the crème-de-la-crème of their community—those with the best English and Arabic language skills and greatest capacity to teach. This was deliberate, for it was these men who translated key texts and instructed later students.[16] Those who were sent in the first three years included future JI leader Zulkarnaen (Aris Sumarsono), DI leader Syawal Yasin, Bali bomber Muchlas (Ali Gufron), and JI strategist Hambali.

New recruits were processed through the "service-base" (Maktab al-Khidmat) in Peshawar set up in 1984 to support foreign mujahidin, and headed by the Palestinian close-confident of Usama bin Ladin, Abdullah Azzam. One of the most important ideologues of the jihadist movement, Azzam re-articulated the concepts first put forth by Sayyid Qutb and linked them to the contemporary context. Most Southeast Asians who went to Azzam's base were familiar with his writing, which had already shaped their thinking.

Almost all of the Southeast Asian mujahidin, and certainly all of those later associated with JI, trained in sections of camps established especially for them by the Saudi-backed leader Abdul Rasul Sayyaf, such as Camp Saddah in the Khumran Agency district of Pakistan.[17] Sayyaf's network was one of the weakest in Afghanistan, but he had some of the best Saudi connections of the Afghan leaders. Furthermore, he understood the needs of his Southeast Asian brothers. He divided Camp Saddah into separate "tribes" (qabilah) or self-sufficient quarters, for those from North Africa, for those from the Middle East, and for those from Southeast Asia. Students in the camps spent part of their time studying contemporary jihadist writings (such as those by Abdullah Azzam) together with classical Salafi texts (such as works by Ibn Taymiyya), and part of

---

[16] International Crisis Group (2002), 5.

[17] International Crisis Group, "Jemaah Islamiyah in South East Asia: Damaged but Still Dangerous," *Asia Report* N°63, 26 August 2003, 3.

43

their time learning how to shoot firearms, construct explosive devices, use mines, conduct guerrilla warfare attacks, and read maps.

After the Soviet withdrawal in 1992, training was shifted to a new camp around Torkham within Afghanistan itself. Interestingly, the Torkham camp was led for several years by Ngruki graduate and key JI strategist Fathur Rahman al-Ghozi. Compared to the local Afghan and Pakistani fighters, the foreign students-cum-fighters saw comparatively little action and made only a relatively minor contribution to the Afghan jihad. This was deliberate, for their mentors had other plans for them, plans that included other jihads.

In late 1992, Sungkar travelled to talk with the mujahidin in Pakistan, asking Southeast Asian fighters to decide whether they stood with him and Ba'asyir or with the old Darul Islam set. These discussions led to the creation of Jemaah Islamiyah, formally established on 1 January 1993. The move to break with Darul Islam and adopt the name Jemaah Islamiyah was inspired by Sungkar's contact with the Gama Islami (al-Gamaat al-Islamiyah), a radical jihadist breakaway faction of Muslim Brotherhood responsible for 1993 World Trade Center bombing in New York City. This shift towards Gama Islami and al-Qa'ida-style global jihadist Islamism caused a split within the extremist community.

In 1996, the group again shifted training grounds, this time moving from Afghanistan to Mindanao, where training occurred in facilities provided by the MILF. The MILF made available a remote corner of their very large Camp Abu Bakar facility. By this time, Jemaah Islamiyah as we now know it had begun to take shape: Abdullah Sungkar and a small group of senior Afghan alumni drafted JI's manual of philosophy and operations, commonly referred to as PUPJI (Pedoman Umum Perjuangan al-Jamaah al-Islamiyah: General Guidelines for the Jemaah Islamiyah Struggle), and JI's network was divided geographically into four *mantiqi*, or spheres of operation. Mantiqi I covered Malaysia and Singapore, and was conceived of as a base for fundraising and recruitment. Mantiqi II initially covered all of Indonesia, but a new sphere of operation, Mantiqi III, was formed to take over responsibility for the island of Borneo (including Indonesian Kalimantan), the island of Sulawesi, and the southern Philippines. Not long afterwards, Mantiqi III became home to JI's major theaters of conflict. Mantiqi IV was tasked with building capability in Australia.

From late 1999 onwards, JI quietly worked to support local jihad in Maluku and Sulawesi. In November 1999, Abdullah Sungkar died of natural causes in Ngruki and the much less charismatic Abu Bakar Ba'asyir became amir in his place. Ba'asyir returned to Indonesia and founded the Majelis Mujahideen Indonesia

(MMI), or Indonesian Mujahedeen Council, which is an umbrella organization of Indonesian Islamist groups, jihadist and non-jihadist alike. The first Mujahidin Congress was held in August 2000 in Yogyakarta. Amongst the guests at the congress were Abdul Wahid Kadungga and the deputy head of Malaysia's Islamist party, PAS. Meanwhile, throughout 2000, JI carried out a series of small to medium terrorist bombings across Indonesia.

The Jihadi Character of Jemaah Islamiyah

In many important respects, JI represents an evolutionary development of Darul Islam; its aims are essentially the same aims as those of Darul Islam with a more global perspective and a strongly developed jihadist ideology. JI leaders have vastly different experiences and training as compared to the Darul Islam leaders of the 1950s. The former's time in Afghanistan and their links with mujahidin across the region and around the world have contributed to their understanding of global struggle. Consequently, they are much more concerned with striking out against both the "near enemy" of the national government (primarily the Indonesian government, but also the Philippines government, and, to the extent that it is possible, the governments of Singapore and Thailand) and the "far enemy" (Western powers) than were the leaders of Darul Islam. But the group's actual willingness to give a high priority to "far enemy" attacks varies greatly within the JI leadership. Charismatic younger leaders such as Noordin Muhammad Top, Azahari, Imam Samudra, and Hambali saw such attacks as an essential obligation. Others, most notably Abu Bakar Ba'asyir, felt strongly that provocative, high risk attacks against foreign interests were at odds with JI's regional aspirations and could not be justified in strategic terms. This latter view now appears to prevail within JI.

As was the case with Darul Islam before it, JI aims to establish a series of religiously pure communities governed by a strict Salafi reading of *sharia*, or Islamic law. It regards the modern Indonesian state, along with all other nation states in the region, to be illegitimate and desires not only the overthrow of these states, but the creation of a new theocratic state in Southeast Asia that unites all Muslims and, ultimately, a global theocratic Islamist state: a caliphate.

Following the writings of Abdullah Azzam and other Salafi jihadi ideologues, JI regards violent, pre-emptive, jihad as an obligation for all Muslims and consequently aims to train mujahidin and engage in jihad, wherever opportunities arise. Some key younger Mantiqi activists, such as Hambali (Riduan Isamuddin), Imam Samudra (Abdul Aziz), and Ali Gufron (Muchlas), are not confident in Ba'asyir's leadership. They feel that, unlike Sungkar, who died in 1999, Ba'asyir lacks conviction in pursuing practical jihad and backs down when faced with risks.[18] They are unhappy with Ba'asyir's decision to join with Irfan Awwas in forming the MMI and aligning that group with pro-establishment (that is to say, recognizing the practical legitimacy of the Indonesian state) political Islamists. This faction's fears were confirmed when, in the wake of the Singapore arrests and revelations about Omar al-Faruq's confessions in the September 2002 issue of *Time* magazine, Ba'asyir argued fervently against proceeding immediately with bombings of Western targets.

At the same time, many within JI were uncomfortable with the large number of Indonesian Muslim victims of the October 2002 bombing in Bali and subsequent attacks. Many also felt that the bombings were counterproductive, causing the Indonesian authorities to clamp-down on JI's local jihad and training operations in Sulawesi.

Regardless of this important internal debate, JI remains unambiguously a jihadi Islamist group constructed on paramilitary lines convinced that it represents part of an army of God fighting a state and a world that has made itself an enemy of God and of true religion. It believes in the necessity and religious legitimacy of using pre-emptive violence when tactically and strategically opportune. It wishes to be seen as a champion of Islam and Muslim interests, and it seeks the support of allies in the broader Islamic community. For operational and ideological reasons, JI knows that it needs to master public relations and win "hearts and minds."

JI has a history of conducting terrorist bombing attacks and will likely conduct further bombings in the future, but this is not the only, or even preferred, method of conducting jihad. Aside from violent jihad, JI also sees itself as an organization committed to *dakwah*, i.e., preaching and teaching. The collapse of the Suharto regime in May 1998 opened up new opportunities for JI to pursue its outreach aims in Indonesia.

The 12 October 2002 bombing in Bali, which targeted foreigners, represented JI's first large-scale attack against the "far enemy." Follow-up bomb attacks on foreign targets took place in 2003, 2004, and 2005, but none achieved the impact of the 2002 bombing. As explained above, these far enemy major attacks were controversial within JI. Ba'asyir evidently did not believe that the 2002 attack made good tactical or strategic sense. The younger bombers, however, did not

---

[18] (ICG Dec 2002:3)

agree with Ba'asyir's MMI strategy. It soon became clear to all within JI that the October 2002 bombings had cost JI dearly, with over three hundred arrested over the ensuing three years.

Despite the arrests, JI continues to be surprisingly resilient even though it would appear that its force strength has declined from a peak of several thousand members down to a mere one thousand or so militants. Recognizing the futility of staging bombing spectaculars, JI now appears awaiting more favorable circumstance in which to re-emerge. Even in Poso, where it had enjoyed considerable success in sustaining sectarian conflict through the first half the decade, the group now finds it difficult to operate.[19]

Popular Support for Jihadi Ideas

The immediate risk environment in Indonesia has improved given JI's current strength, but the global environment remains conducive to the development of jihadist terrorism and the recruiting of a new generation of activists. Credible political Islamists (especially the Prosperous Justice Party, or PKS) and social movements (especially Hizbut Tahrir Indonesia) have helped establish the legitimacy of the Islamist cause. At the same time, complex synergies that arise between non-violent radical Islamist activists and semi-underground jihadi elements, such as some associated with MMI, create spaces for the promotion of jihadi ideas.[20] The vast majority of Indonesians want to move on and forget about terrorism, some aspects of jihadi thought have increased in appeal and garnered support.

Indications of increased support for key jihadi ideas can be found in national surveys by the Center for the Study of Islam and Society (Pusat Pengkajian Islam dan Masyarakat, or PPIM) at the National Islamic University in Jakarta (UIN Syarif Hidayatullah), Indonesia's premier Islamic center of learning. PPIM's 2007

---

[19] These issues are comprehensively dealt with in: International Crisis Group, "Indonesia: Tackling Radicalism in Poso," *Asia Briefing* N°75, 22 January 2008. It is instructive to note, however, that one of the key JI trainers—a graduate of the full three-year course in Camp Saddah and founder of the JI training camps in Ambon in 1999—is the son of one of the men who, half a century ago, attempted the assassination of president Sukarno at Cikini in 1957. This was drawn from an interview with the author, Jakarta, November 2007.

[20] On Hizbut Tahrir Hizbut Tahrir in Indonesia refer to: Greg Fealy, "Hizbut Tahrir in Indonesia: Seeking a "Total" Muslim Identity", in *Islam and Political Violence: Muslim Diaspora and Radicalism in the West*, ed. Shahram Akbarzadeh and Fethi Mansouri (London and New York: I.B. Tauris, 2007): 151-64; and Agus Salim, *Transnational Political Islam: The Rise of Hizb al-Tahrir in Indonesia*, unpublished MA Thesis, Monash University (2007).

survey report, entitled "Attitudes, Behaviour and Religious Violence in Indonesia (Findings of a National Survey)," contained some very interesting results that suggest approval for the literalist readings of the *hudud* ordinances within *sharia* law associated with Salafi jihadist groups.[21] Under the heading of "support for Islamism," it was reported that 57.7 percent of respondents agreed with the punishment of death by stoning for adulterers and 30 percent agreed with amputating the hands of convicted thieves.[22] Similarly, 18.1 percent expressed support for the notion that apostates should be killed.[23] While a quarter of respondents (25.2 percent) were ready to fight as mujahidin in Poso, half of the respondents (49 percent) agreed that, as a matter of principle, Muslims were obliged to fight in Poso to defend other Muslims.[24] A third of respondents (32.8 percent) viewed the American actions in Iraq and Afghanistan as attacks on Muslims and as many as one in six (16.1 percent) said that the 11 September 2001 attacks could be justified retrospectively on the basis of the U.S. response in Iraq and Afghanistan. A full 23.1 percent expressed willingness to join in jihad in defense of Muslims in Iraq and Afghanistan. Finally, one in five (20.5 percent) agreed that the 2002 Bali bombings were justified.

A second PPIM survey in 2007, entitled "Assessment of Social and Political Attitudes in Indonesian Schools: Madrasah and Pesantren Directors and Students," examined the views of religious teachers (ulama: kyai, and ustadz) and senior students in a sample of the 20,000 pesantren and thousands of madrasah associated with Muhammadiyah and NU.[25] This study shows that Islamic teachers and students are much more conservative in their views and convictions than Indonesian society as a whole. Schools such al-Mu'min Pesantren in Ngruki naturally represent the conservative end of the spectrum and are not representative of Indonesian pesantren in general. Nevertheless, the results of this survey suggest that their views are not held in isolation. For instance, while 30 percent of ordinary people surveyed expressed support for the *hudud* punishment of amputation, twice as many (59.1 percent) of religious schooling respondents voiced support.[26] Similarly, twice as many of the

---

[21] PPIM UIN Jakarta, *Sikap dan Perilaku Kekerasan Keagamaan di Indonesia (Temuan Survey Nasional)*, http://www.ppim.or.id/doc/file/20070607091626.pdf

[22] Ibid., 12.

[23] Ibid., 10. "Muslim yang keluar dari Islam (murtad) harus dibunuh (18,1%)."

[24] Ibid., 7.

[25] Jamhari and Jajat Burhanudi, *Assessment of Social and Political Attitudes in Indonesian Schools (madrasah and Pesantren Directors and Students)*, (PPIM UIN Jakarta) http://www.ppim.or.id/doc/file/20070530032238.pdf

[26] Ibid., 21.

respondents in religious schools (67.0 percent) said that they believed that the American actions in Iraq and Afghanistan represented attacks on Islam.[27] When it came to the proposition that "Western countries, primarily the United States and Great Britain, are the root cause of religious violence in Muslim countries (such as bombings in Indonesia and in Middle Eastern countries)," four out five (80 percent) agreed, whereas only one in ten (10.1 percent) were critical of Usama bin Ladin and prepared to agree that he was an "actor of violence in the world."[28] A remarkable two out of three of these respondents at Islamic educational institutions affirmed that they "support the foundation of an Islamic state and the implementation of sharia as advocated by Darul Islam (DI), Negara Islam Indonesia (NII), Majlis Mujahidin Indonesia (MMI), Front Pembela Islam (FPI) and Laskar Jihad (LJ)."[29]

Clearly, there is much deeper support for jihadi ideas within Indonesia's *pesantren*, *madrasah* and Islamic colleges than one might hope. For the reasons outlined at the beginning of this chapter, it seems likely that this apparent support for radical jihadi Islamism is a product of long-established social conservatism in NU and theological conservatism within Muhammadiyah.

---

[27] Ibid., 28.

[28] Ibid.

[29] Ibid., 20. On Laskar Jihad refer tp Laskar Jihad see: Noorhaidi Hasan, *Laskar Jihad: Islam, Militancy, and the Quest for Identity in Post-New Order Indonesia* (Ithaca: Cornell Southeast Asia Program, 2006); also refer to Saiful Umam, "Radical Muslims in Indonesia: the Case of Ja'far Umar Thalib and Laskar Jihad", Explorations in Southeast Asian Studies, vol.6, no.1 (Spring 2006). For broader studies of Laskar Jihad, other jihadi militia and militant Islamism refer to: Zachary Abuza, *Political Islam and Violence in Indonesia* (London: Routledge, 2007); Greg Fealy, "Militant Java-based Islamist Movements", in *A Handbook of Terrorism and Insurgency in Southeast Asia*, ed. Andrew Tan (Cheltenham: Edward Elgar, 2007): 63-76; Greg Fealy, "Half a Century of Violent Jihad in Indonesia: An Historical and Ideological Comparison of Darul Islam and Jema'ah Islamiyah", in *Islamic Terrorism in Indonesia: Myths and Realities*, ed. Marika Vicziany and David Wright-Neville, CSEAS Annual Indonesia Lecture Series, number 26 (Melbourne: Monash Asia Institute, 2005): 15-31; Greg Fealy and Anthony Bubalo, *Between the Global and the Local: Islamism, the Middle East, and Indonesia*, Analysis Paper No. 9, The Brookings Project on U.S. Policy Towards the Islamic World (Washington D.C.: The Saban Center for Middle East Policy at The Brookings Institution, 2005); Greg Fealy and Aldo Borgu, *Local Jihad: Radical Islam and Terrorism in Indonesia*, (Canberra: Australian Strategic Policy Institute, 2005); and Martin Van Bruinessen, "Genealogies of Islamic Radicalism in Post-Suharto Indonesia", *South East Asia Research* 10, no. 2 (2002): 117–24. On FPI see: Jajang Jahroni et.al., "Defending the Majesty of Islam: Indonesia's Front Pembela Islam (FPI) 1998-2003", Studia Islamika vol. 11, no. 2 (2004): 197-56; and Ian Douglas Wilson, "The Changing Contours of Organised Violence in Post New Order Indonesia", Murdoch University *Asia Research Centre Working Paper* No. 118 (April 2005) .

Jihadi Publishing in Indonesia

Publishing, both through conventional print-media and online, has become an increasingly important part of jihadi activism in Indonesia. As was noted above, between 1982 and 1986, several dozen key jihadi texts by seminal intellectuals such as Hassan al-Banna, Maududi, Sayyid Qutb, and Ali Shariati were made available to broad readerships in Indonesia in affordable translations appearing in bookstores all across the country. In the decades since then, all major works of jihadi thinkers such as Abdullah Azzam, Abdul Qadir bin Abdul Aziz, and Abu Muhammad al-Maqdisi, have been translated and published in relatively large print-runs. At the same time, tabloid publications popularising jihadi ideas, analysis, myths, and conspiracy theories, such as *Sabili* magazine, have enjoyed some of the highest circulations of any Indonesia print-media titles and have done much to socialize and normalize jihadi thought.

Ironically, the arrest, prosecution, and incarceration of several hundred JI activists over the past half-dozen years coincided with a boom in jihadi publishing. It appears as if JI has, for the time being at least, reorientated itself away from terrorist violence and towards *dakwah* and publishing. This was documented in detail by the International Crisis Group Jakarta office team led by Sidney Jones. A February 2008 report entitled *Indonesia: Jemaah Islamiyah's Publishing Industry* concludes that:[30]

> The publishing venture demonstrates JI's resilience and the extent to which radical ideology has developed roots in Indonesia. The Indonesian government should monitor these enterprises more closely, but they may be playing a useful role by channelling JI energies into waging jihad through the printed page rather than acts of violence.
>
> Examining the titles printed permits tracking of a lively internal debate within JI over the desirability of al-Qaeda tactics....[31]

In September 2006, MMI partnered with the Ahlus Suffah Foundation and the An-Nabawy Islamic Study Center to publish *Risalah Mujahidin* (*Stories of the Mujahidin*). The Arafah Group, one of the leading publishers directly linked with

---

[30] International Crisis Group, "Indonesia: Jemaah Islamiyah's Publishing Industry," *Asia Report* N°147, 28 February 2008. Most of the publishing activities briefly outlined here are examined in depth in this ICG report.
[31] Ibid., 'Executive Summary'.

JI, publishes a similar but different magazine called *Ar-Risalah*. Another magazine published by members of MMI, *Al Muhajrun*, focuses particularly on stories of jihad in the Middle East. MMI also has its own publishing house, Wihdah Press. Hizb ut-Tahrir Indonesia publishes several lines of books, as well as the tabloid newspaper *Suara Islam* and the monthly magazine *al-Wa'ie*.

Most of the publishing ventures directly linked to JI are head-quartered in Solo and led by graduates of Ngruki's Pesantren al-Mu'min. They are often associated with the Islamic Publishers Union (SPI), and their publications are listed on the SPI website at: solobook.wordpress.com.

In addition to JI websites, the Muslim Brotherhood movement in Indonesia, which is closely associated with the PKS, runs the popular website www.eraintermedia.com. MMI members are also active in a variety of internet publishing initiatives including MMI's official website, www.majelismujahidin.or.id, and the related website www.laskarmujahidin.wordpress.com. Some websites, such as www.anshar.net, founded by Agung Prabowo and associated with jihadi internet specialist Fais Indrawan, focus on translating jihadi texts between Arabic and Indonesian. Anshar.net was also closely linked to JI masterminds Noordin Muhammad Top and Imam Samudra, with the latter running the website for a time in mid-2005 from his laptop whilst in Krobokan prison in Central Java.

Key publishing houses linked to jihadi circles include Pustaka Al Wustho, associated with 1992 Ngruki graduates Junaidi Afwan and Hawin Murtadho. One of the first JI publishing houses was al-Alaq run by Ikhsan Miarso, the former leader of JI's Solo subdivision and an early graduate of JI/DI's full three-year training program in Afghanistan/Pakistan. Al-Alaq began publishing in 1994 when it translated the works of Abdullah Azzam and today is associated with classic jihadi texts and related academic volumes of a serious nature. It has published works by the Saudi cleric Sa'id bin Ali bin Wahf al-Qahtani and the Syrian jihadi writer Abu Bashur al-Tartousi.

The Arafah Group has come to publishing relatively recently. In 2006, the JI publisher published its first title under the Media Islamika imprint, an imprint devoted exclusively to jihadi texts, when it published Abdullah Azzam's *Join the Caravan of Martyrs*. It then published the works of Saudi cleric Salman al-Audah and Egyptian jihadi mastermind, and close associate of Ayman al-Zawahiri, Abdul Qadir bin Abdul Aziz. It has since published works by Ayman al-Zawahiri himself and by Yusuf al-'Uyairi, the former bodyguard of Usama bin

Ladin who was killed by the Saudi authorities in 2003. Some of the Arafah Group publications have introductions by Abu Bakar Ba'asyir.

A second JI publisher is the Al-Qowam group, which was founded in 1999 and is led by JI activist Hawin Murtadlo who graduated from Ngruki in 1991. Al-Qowam publications focus on Salafi piety rather than politics or related jihadi matters and as a result it enjoys a good reputation in non-jihadi, Salafi circles. This is an important consideration because it remains the case in Indonesia as elsewhere that many Salafists are opposed to Jihadi terrorism.[32]

The third major publishing group associated directly with JI is the Al Aqwam Group, which is led by Bambang Sukirno. Sukirno achieved early commercial success with the publication in September 2004 of Imam Samudra's curiously titled *Aku Melawan Terroris* (*I Fight Terrorists*), in which the convicted JI terrorist justifies his role in the 2002 Bali bombing. Sukirno also publishes the popular jihadi monthly magazine *an-Najah* and, in 2005, he published Abu Muhammad al-Maqdisi's polemical *Saudi in the Eyes of an al-Qaeda member* and Saudi dissident Safar al-Wawali's *Awaiting the Death of Israel*.

Conclusion

Several leading JI figures have begun to make their mark as jihadi authors. One of the first significant books written by a JI activist is Samudra's *Aku Melawan Terroris* which has sold more than 12,000 copies—making it a best seller in Indonesian publishing terms. More recently, Mukhlas, with the assistance of the Muslim Lawyers Team (TPM) has produced his first book. Nevertheless, as was noted at the outset of this chapter, Indonesia, which leads the world in progressive Islamic thought, has yet to produce significant, original, jihadi intellectuals. Rather, Indonesia's particular genius in this area is the way in which diverse schools of thought, such as those associated with the Muslim Brotherhood, with the ideas of Maududi and of India's Deobandi movement, and ideas associated with Saudi Salafism/Wahhabism, which in the Middle East are pitched against each other despite their broad Salafi doctrinal common world view, are brought together in a constructive synthesis.

There remains limited support in Indonesia for al-Qa'ida's brand of jihadist violence, although even this is more substantial than expected. There is remarkably broad support for the sort of issues being championed by Abu Bakar

---

[32] This matter is treated at length in: ICG, "Indonesia Backgrounder: Why Salafism and Terrorism Mostly Don't Mix" ", *Asia Report* N°83 (13 September 2004).

Ba'asyir in MMI and other forums. Consequently, so long as he and other jihadi leaders confine themselves to strong rhetoric whilst avoiding indiscriminate violence, their ideas may continue to find support within Indonesian society.

The Influence of Transnational Jihadist Ideology on Islamic Extremist Groups in the Philippines: The Cases of the Abu Sayyaf Group and the Rajah Solaiman Movement

Renato Cruz De Castro

Introduction

Prior to the 1990s, insurgency and terrorism in Southeast Asia, though rampant and endemic, were largely local or regional in scope. Linkages between various terrorist and insurgent groups were relatively weak, and most of the groups traditionally operated only in their own country or region, focusing on domestic issues and grievances. As a case in point, the various Islamic insurgent groups in the Philippines in the 1970s and 1980s were confined mainly to the Muslim dominated regions in Mindanao, where they waged a secessionist campaign against the central government. Southeast Asia was then a hotbed of Muslim militants whose concerns were parochial, not transnational. While the militant groups generated concern because of their regular resort to violence, they posed minimal threat to international order and security.

All of this changed in the 1990s, as the region witnessed the emergence of religious-inspired and transnational insurgents and terrorist groups. Rather than focusing on the overthrow of secular governments in the region, these new actors worked toward the establishment of a supranational Islamic state ruled by Sharia law. Inspired by the socio-political ideology of Islamism, these new groups have merged "religion and politics (*din wa dawla*)" together in a way that directly challenges the Western secular model of governance. More specifically, they have adopted and internalized the late Egyptian poet Sayyid Qutb's slogan "Islam is the solution" in an effort to inspire political movements against secular Western-type governments in Islamic countries. They do this with of the expectation of inevitably convincing the West that an Islamic world driven by Islamic values can and should have autonomy and legitimacy.[1] They have also forged, or are in the process of forging, transnational links both within the region and, significantly, with global Islamic terrorist movements like al-Qa'ida. Meanwhile, the jihadist agenda continues to spread throughout the region through tapes, sermons, booklets, leaflets, newspapers, journals, books, and small groups of indoctrinators that traverse the Southeast Asia states.

---

[1] Andrew Harvey, Ian Sullivan, and Ralph Groves, "A Clash of Systems: An Analytical Framework to Demystify the Radical Islamic Threat," *Parameters* 35, no. 3 (Autumn 2005), 76.

Despite the general growth in fundamentalism in the region, the degree of militancy and associated ideological sophistication of the different Islamic extremist groups varies significantly throughout Southeast Asia, largely as a result of country-specific factors. Indeed, the socio-political context, characterized by pre-existing conflicts vulnerable to the influence of jihadist views, greatly affects the absorption of fundamentalist ideologies in each Southeast Asian society. While various extremist groups in Southeast Asia have the motives and means to forge transnational links with jihadist groups abroad, they are constrained by their own internal context, instrumentalist agenda, and other factors such as individual differences and factional rivalries.

This chapter examines the presence and the depth of jihadi ideology among Islamic militant groups in the Philippines, focusing on the Abu Sayyaf Group (ASG) and the Raja Suleiman Movement (RSM). Evidence suggests that both groups have a desire to link up to the transnational jihadi movement, thereby representing a substantial threat both inside and outside of the region. At the same time, however, the chapter concludes that the influence of jihadist ideology on the Filipino-Muslim society is minimal because of the distinct nature of local Islamic resurgence and the widely-held view that ASG and RSM are marginalized extremist groups operating at the fringes of the mainstream Islamic movement in the Philippines.

The Abu Sayyaf Group: A Jihadist Ideology in a Bandit Group?

Background

Historically, the establishment of the Abu Sayyaf Group may be traced back to the Afghan War, when hundreds of Filipino Muslims went to Pakistan and Afghanistan to join the mujahidin. Among them was Abdurajak Abubakar Janjalani, a Tausog from the island of Basilan.[2] As a member of the Moro National Liberation Front (MNLF), Janjalani went to Pakistan in 1987.[3] While

---

[2] Janjalani allegedly fought in the International Islamic Brigade while in Afghanistan. See Mark Turner, "The Management of Violence in a Conflict Organization: The Case of the Abu Sayyaf," *Public Organization Review* 3, no. 4 (December 2003), 388.

[3] The MNLF was originally a nationalist and secessionist organization with an Islamic coloring rather than a movement inspired by religious fervor. The absence of any strong leanings towards Islam by the MNLF could be attributed to a mélange of antithetical forces in its political structures. The organization was a marriage of clashing political forces, and an alliance of conservative Filipino Muslim elite and Marxist-inspired young radicals led by Nur Misuari, a former professor at the University of the Philippines. Its primary political objective was to

there, he met Usama bin Ladin and befriended such figures as Ramzi Yousef and Abdur Rab Rasul Sayaaf, a religious scholar. He was also exposed to, and influenced by, Middle East-Sunni jihadist ideology, including the following principles: 1) commitment to the renewal of an Umma by a return to Islam's fundamentalist roots; 2) advocacy of jihad in the defense of the faith; 3) establishment of Allah's sovereignty—*al Hakmiyah*—over the whole of humanity; 4) revival of the caliphate going back to the fourth rightly successor of the prophet, al-Rashidun; and 5) creation of a Muslim Umma based on *salafiyyah* (Islamic puritanical beliefs).[4]

By the time of the Soviet withdrawal from Afghanistan, Janjalani had become committed to waging a jihad back home in Mindanao to create a pure Islamic state based on Salafi Wahhabism.[5] Thus, upon his return to Basilan, Janjalani became disenchanted with what he viewed as the moderate aims and tactics of the mainstream MNLF and, in 1991, Janjalani and seven of his followers broke from MNLF to form ASG.[6] While the group initially consisted of just twenty members, primarily Muslim volunteers who fought in Afghanistan, ASG eventually attracted hundreds of recruits, as Janjalani was able to persuade a number of MNLF provincial commanders that their group was not waging a real jihad against the Christians. Moreover, in the early 1990s, ASG received financial and material support from foreign sources, including al-Qa'ida, which helped to bolster its capabilities.[7]

Since its early days, the estimated number of ASG fighters has varied from a

---

liberate the Filipino Muslims from the terror, oppression and tyranny of the Filipino Christians, and to establish an independent and secular Muslim state by means of an armed struggle. The MNLF got support from Muammar Qaddafi of Libya and from the governor of Sabah, Malaysia, who both supplied arms and provided training and other forms of aid to these young Filipino Muslims.

[4] Philippine Marines, *Doctrinal Extracts: Abu Sayyaf* (Makati City: Philippine Marines, date unknown), 39-40.

[5] Zachary Abuza, "Al Qaeda Comes to Southeast Asia," in *Terrorism and Violence in Southeast Asia: Transnational Challenges and Regional Stability*, ed. Paul J. Smith (New York: M.E. Sharpe, Inc., 2005), 42; Zachary Abuza, "Tentacles of Terror: Al-Qeada's Southeast Asian Network," *Contemporary Southeast Asia* (2002), 14.

[6] Turner, 388.

[7] See Larry Niksch, "Abu Sayyaf: Target of Philippine-US Anti-Terrorism Cooperation," *Congressional Research Service* (Washington, DC: The Library of Congress, 25 January 2002), 4; Turner, 395-96; Abuza (2002), 14.

minimum of 100 to a maximum of 3000.[8] ASG members are picked from a restricted and specific ethno-linguistic group (mainly the Tausogs and some Yakans). Thus, it operates on the basis of the cultural values of the majority group, in this case, the Tausog's violence-prone culture.[9] This policy does limit ASG's ability to recruit Muslims from other ethnic groups, however, internal cohesion and coordination are facilitated by trust, shared values, and norms drawn on the narrow basis of tribal kinship.

ASG's principal objective is to unify "all sectors of the predominantly Muslim provinces in the [southern Philippines] and establish an Islamic state governed by the Sharia in that region, a state where Muslims can follow Islam in its purest and strictest form as the only path to Allah."[10] In some ways, this goal overlaps with the aim of MNLF and its more radical offshoot, the Moro Islamic Liberation Front (MILF).[11] Indeed, ASG, MNLF, and MILF have long competed for

---

[8] Jeffrey Bale, "The Abu Sayyaf Group in its Philippine and International Contexts," (Unpublished monograph, Center for Non-Proliferation Studies, Monterey Institute of International Studies, date unknown), 32. See also Niksch, 2-3.

[9] Bale, 25-27.

[10] Ibid., 34.

[11] Bale, 34. The MILF is an offshoot resulting from a leadership split within the MNLF. This breakaway group was headed by the late Hashim Salamat. In contrast to the MNLF's call for a Moro nation (*bangsa*), the MILF espouses Islam as the basis of its struggle against the Philippine state. Unlike the secular goal of the MNLF, the MILF pursues for the establishment an Islamic state in southern Philippines. The MILF advocates a four-point program of Islamization, organizational strengthening, military build up, and economic self-sufficiency. The MILF, under Salamat, emphasizes its Islamic orientation in terms of goals, organizational structure, armed struggle, and links with the external world. While the MNLF draws most of its supporters from the Tausogs of the Sulu Archipelago, the MILF is mostly made up of Maguindanaos, and Iranun ethnic groups, and some Maranaos. Prior to its capture by the Armed Forces of the Philippines in July 2000, the MILF made Camp Abubakar into a self-contained and fortified Islamic community with a mosque, a religious school, a military training camp, an arms factory, a solar power source, sophisticated communication equipment, family housing, markets, a fruit nursery, and agricultural plots. The camp served as a model, living showcase of an Islamic state and society that the MILF eventually hopes to establish throughout Mindanao. The Philippine government estimates that the MILF has some 12,000 current armed members—many of them could be potential recruits for any transnational terrorist groups like JI or al-Qa'ida. Given its present military strength, large popular support base, control of "liberated areas" in Mindanao, and close operational links with al-Qa'ida and JI, the MILF is poised as a potent threat to the Philippine government and to the U.S.

Although the MILF has been accused collaborating with Southeast Asian transnational terrorist groups, including the JI and the Abu Sayyaf, the group's leadership has denied the charge, maintaining since 2002 that the organization has cut off ties with all terrorist groups to pave the

supporters among the Muslim population of Mindanao.[12] Still, ASG has distinguished itself from MNLF and MILF along two significant fronts: the first being ideological, and the second being operational.

ASG's Ideology

The first way that ASG distinguishes itself from MNLF and MILF is that the former is noticeably more aggressive than the latter two in its inclusion of Islam in its political agenda. For instance, ASG not only seeks an independent Muslim state in the southern Philippines, but also advocates ridding Sulu and Mindanao of all non-Muslims, by force if necessary. Moreover, ASG explicitly tries to define its ideological and operational agenda as being intimately tied to an integrated effort aimed at asserting the global dominance of Islam through armed jihad.[13] Indeed, when Janjalani formed the group, his intention was to form a Muslim core group of mujahidin committed to jihad *Fi-Sabil-lillah*, a "struggle in the

---

way for formal peace talks with the Philippine government. The MILF set three conditions before it would negotiate with the Philippine government: a) the talks should be mediated by the Organisation of The Islamic Conference (OIC) or by an OIC member country; b) both parties should comply with the terms of past agreements; and c) that the talks should be held in a foreign soil. All three conditions were accepted by the Arroyo administration, and in 2001, the MILF signed the Tripoli Agreement on Peace with the Philippine government. The agreement provides for an incremental and piece-meal approach to the peace negotiations, as it emphasizes the crafting of confidence-building measures before contentious issues of political nature can be gradually be resolved by both sides. The agreement also lays down the modalities for the cessation of hostilities and the creation of restraining arrangements for the MILF and the AFP. To ensure that these rules are observed, an International Monitoring Team, headed by Malaysia, has been convened to be deployed in the conflict-affected areas. Currently, both parties have constituted various technical committees to resolve numerous pressing issues in the peace talks. Nevertheless, despite the on going negotiations, there is a lingering suspicion that hard-line MILF members still maintain their links with militant Muslim groups by giving terrorist training, sharing resources and combatants, and providing refuge to other extremists on the run from government offensive. See Jacques Bertran, "Peace and Conflict in the Southern Philippines: Why the 1996 Peace Agreement is Fragile?," *Pacific Affairs* 73, no. 3 (Spring 2000), 3, http://proquest.umi.com/pqdweb?index=31&sid=1&vinst=PROD&fmt=3&startpage=-1&cl; Mohd Shafie Apdal and Carlyle A. Thayer, "Security, Political Terrorism and Militant Islam in Southeast Asia," *Trends in Southeast Asia Series* 7 (Singapore: Institute of Southeast Asian Studies, August 2003); Jim Gomez, "Extremist Groups in the Philippines Forming Alliances," *Associated Press* (12 March 2005), 1, http://www.chron.com/cs/CDA/ssistroy.mpl/world/3081439; Paul Alexander, "Philippines Sees Terrorism Links Growing," *Associated Press* (2 March 2005), 1-2, http://seattlepi.nwsource.com/national/apasia_story.asp?category=1; Abuza (2002), 11-14.
[12] Turner, 388.
[13] Peter Chalk, "Militant Islamic Extremism," *Terrorism and Violence in Southeast Asia: Transnational Challenges to States and Regional Stability*, ed. Paul J. Smith (New York: M.E. Sharpe, 2005), 20.

cause of Allah" or fighting and dying for the cause of Islam.[14] He also denounced the Filipino *ulama* (Muslin scholars) for their limited knowledge of Islam compared with their counter parts in West Asia.[15]

Perhaps the greatest insight into the ideology of ASG comes from a thirty-page pamphlet entitled *Jihad in the Philippines* that was taken from an ASG camp in Basilan. Pseudonymously written by Abu Ramadan, *Jihad in the Philippines* contains some of ASG's main ideas regarding the conduct and rationale of jihad in the Philippine context. Largely based on the ideas of the late Dr. Abdullah Yusuf Azzam and the lectures of Abdurajak Abubakar Janjalani, who was killed in 1998, the pamphlet argues that a continuing jihad is an integral part of Islam. For instance, it exhorts: "Jihad must not be abandoned until Allah alone is worshipped (by mankind). Jihad continues until Allah's Word is raised high. Jihad until all oppressed people are freed. Jihad to protect our occupied land. Jihad is the way of everlasting glory."[16] The pamphlet further argues that jihad is an obligation of every Muslim and that any Muslim who denies its sanctity should be considered as a *kufr* (infidel). It enumerates the forms of jihad as: 1) *Maliki Figh*—when Muslims are to fight against the kufr to advance Islam; 2) *Shafi'ee figh*—making the utmost effort in fighting in the path of Allah; 3) *Hanbali figh*—fighting against the infidels or non-believers; and 4) *Hanafi figh*—fighting in the path of Allah by one's life, wealth, and speech.[17] The pamphlet also warns that any government that opposes jihad will surely be defeated. Interestingly, it contends that jihad should not only be waged to free Mindanao from the hold of an infidel government, but also to install an Islamic government all over the Philippines.

The alleged author of *Jihad in the Philippines*, Abu Ramadan, claims that all Muslims who have responded positively to Allah's call for the creation of a Sharia in the Philippines could be regarded as a mujahidin. He quotes liberally from the Qur'an to rationalize the mujahidin's sole purpose to "wage the jihad against the infidels until they embrace Islam."[18] If the mujahidin get killed in the process, the author affirms that the Qur'an promises them that "Allah himself

---

[14] Rommel C. Banlaoi, *Al-Harakatul Al Islamya: Essays on the Abu Sayyaf* (Quezon City: The Alternative Pool of Printing Service, forthcoming book), 46.

[15] Ibid.

[16] Abu Ramadan, *Jihad in the Philippines* (2000), Author's Introduction.

[17] Ibid.

[18] Ibid., 13.

will guide them and admit them to Paradise."[19] By emphasizing the significance of the mujahidin in the jihad, the author is clearly influenced by Azzam's notion of an *al-Qa'ida al-suhbah,* or the vanguard of the strong, who would act independently in setting the example for the rest of the Islamic word and presumably galvanize the Umma against the kufr. The author also proffers a nihilist view of the mujahidin in the pursuit of jihad. In contrast to the strict ideational code of other insurgent groups like the New People's Army, the author of the ASG pamphlet maintains that mujahidin should never be swayed by any ideology, as an ideology is simply the ideas of other human beings. Rather, they must be true to fundamentalist Islam and must use all absolute and radical means to eradicate the evils of society and impose the *sunnah* of the Prophet.

The pamphlet further justifies tactics such as the use of terrorism and banditry to exact revenge on the Philippine government for invading and plundering the Muslim societies. Similarly, the author rationalizes kidnap-for-ransom as a means of generating funds to purchase arms for the jihad. Indeed, he praises the mujahidin for being criminals since they never follow man-made constitutions, laws, and norms; rather, they should operate according to the Qur'an and Sharia. These teachings may in part account for the ASG's ruthless and bandit-like behavior, described in the following section. Following his rejection of secular law, Abu Ramadan advises that Islamic warriors never accept any peace agreements with the government, as their ultimate goal is the overthrow the evil existing system of governance.[20] The author enthuses:

> Citizens of this country (the Philippines)! You have only one choice now! That is to get back to the religion of your forefathers which is Islam and join the Mujahedeen in their struggle Jihad fii Sabillah! Fighting the cause of Allah, destroy this Haram man-made systems (*sic*) of Government and reestablish our Islamic Government using the Sharia—the Divine Law.[21]

Jihad in the Philippines also lists the essential qualities of the ideal amir, the leader of the mujahidin. Specifically, this amir should be both a pious imam and a fearless warrior, religious, frugal, honest, and brave; he should not be afraid of becoming a Shaheed (martyr).

---

[19] Ibid., XXX
[20] Ibid., 22.
[21] Ibid., 33.

Finally, the author of the pamphlet asserts that jihad in the Philippines should have a transnational dimension. Such a struggle must never be confined to a secessionist goal, but must be tasked with spreading the faith throughout the world and annihilating man-made laws and governments. The author contends:

> The Mujahedeen will not fight for the sake of the Bangsamoro only or any tribe or nationality. Islam has no borders, no tribalism, no nationalism, or any ism! The Mujahedeen are fighting the enemies of Allah for the sole purpose to implement the divine laws, which is the Shariah, legislated by God the Almighty Allah for the entire human race, applicable to Muslims and non-Muslims, it is a perfect law! For Allah is perfect.[22]

ASG's Tactics

The second way that ASG distinguishes itself from MNLF and MILF is through its choice of tactics. Perhaps most prominently, ASG follows an interpretation of Islam that justifies the killing of infidels and depriving them of their possessions.[23] Accordingly, ASG, unlike MNLF and MILF, has rejected any prospect of negotiating a peaceful settlement to the Mindanao conflict with the Philippine government. Furthermore, ASG has engaged in a variety of criminal activities, including kidnapping for ransom; murder; hostage-takings; extortion of peasants, businessmen, and fishermen; the cultivation of marijuana; and rape.[24]

ASG did not always rely on criminal tactics, and it is believed that the change in its behavior over the past decade is largely a result of a decline in foreign support and the death of Abubakar Janjalani. As mentioned above, ASG received financial and material support from foreign sources, including al-Qa'ida, in the early 1990s.[25] ASG's ties to al-Qa'ida were severed, however, following Ramzi

---

[22] Ibid., 23.

[23] Ibid., 35.

[24] For more detailed accounts of the Abu Sayyaf's violent activities in Mindanao, see Turner, 388-390; Christopher A. Parrinello, "Enduring Freedom," *Military Intelligence Professional Bulletin* 28, no. 2 (April-June 2002), 3-4, http://proquest.umi.com/pqdweb?index=1&sid=3&srchmode=1&vinst=PROD&fmt=4&st; Zachary Abuza, *Militant Islam in Southeast Asia: Crucible of Terror* (Boulder, Colorado; London, UK: Lynne Rienner Publishers, 2003), 111-13.

[25] See Niksch, 14.

Yousef's arrest in the Philippines in early 1995.[26] Janjalani was killed only a few years in later, in 1998, by Armed Forces of the Philippines (AFP). Following the assumption of ASG's command by Janjalani's brother, Khadaffy, and Ghalib Andang, ASG began regularly committing common crimes such as kidnappings and extortions. These operations grew in April 2000, when ASG began targeting foreigners for the purpose of extracting ransom payments. The first such operation involved the raiding of a tourist resort in the Malaysian state of Sabah and the kidnapping of twenty-one foreigners. In May of the following year, the group again raided a tourist resort, this time on the Philippine island of Palawan, where ASG kidnapped twenty people, including three Americans. In both of these kidnapping cases, the Abu Sayyaf Group killed some hostages and released the others after ransoms were paid.

Such activities continue today; for instance, in early January 2009, ASG militants kidnapped three representatives of the International Committee of the Red Cross (ICRC) in Patikul, Sulu. The three representatives arrived on island to observe humanitarian operations in the province but were intercepted and kidnapped by the militants. ASG immediately announced that three ICRC representatives (one Swiss, one Italian, and one Filipina) were in their custody and demanded a stop to police and military operations in Sulu and a ransom of Php 5 million (US $250,000) for the safe release of the hostages.[27] The following month, ASG operatives abducted three teachers in Zamboanga City in the main island of Mindanao and two employees of a lending company in Basilan Island.[28]

The Rajah Solaiman Movement

Background

Another Islamist group that takes up the cudgels for the transnational jihadist movement is the Raja Solaiman Movement, an association of Christian converts to Islam. Often associated with the *Balik-Islam* (Return to Islam) Movement, RSM is composed of Filipino-Christians who converted to Islam as a result of the Philippine government policy of sending Overseas Filipino Workers to the Middle East beginning in the 1970s. RSM was organized in 2001 by Ahmed Santos, who encouraged a group of twenty Muslim converts to undergo jihad

---

[26] Ibid., 4.

[27] "ICRC Halts Mindanao Work," *Filipino Reporter* 37, no. 7, (23 January – 29 January 2009), 1, 10.

[28] "Two More Abducted in Basilan," *The Filipino Express* 23, no. 6 (6 February – 12 February 2009), 1, 21.

training in the organization's camp in Luzon.[29] The trainees were shown films about Islamic jihads in Iraq, Bosnia, Mindanao, and Indonesia, as well as footage regarding the massacre of Muslim women and children in various conflicts throughout the world.[30] After each film exhibition, Santos lectured on how Islam could be purified in the Philippines. Aside from sessions on the global dimension of jihad, the trainees also learned bomb-making and urban guerrilla warfare. Allegedly, the indoctrination highlighted martyrdom missions (specifically suicide bombings) by repeated exposure to the message that the greatest sacrifice is giving one's life to Allah and Islam.[31] After a month of training, five RSM members pledged to execute a suicide mission to assassinate President Gloria Macapagal Arroyo using a truck bomb in May 2002, but the plot was disrupted by security forces.[32] The following year, RSM established links with the Abu Sayaff Group and Jamiya Islamiya (JI).[33]

---

[29] Rommel Banlaoi, "Radical Muslim Terrorism in the Philippines," *A Handbook of Terrorism and Insurgency in Southeast Asia*, ed. Andrew T. H. Tan (Cheltenham, UK; MA, USA: Edward Elgar Publications, 2007), 217.

[30] Details of the 2001 training session were provided by Rommel Banlaoi, "Muslim Converts Terrorism and Political Violence: The Rajah Solaiman Islamic Movement," originally presented during the Council of Asian Terrorism Research, Philippine Plaza Hotel, Manila, 27-29 March 2007.

[31] Banlaoi (2007a), 214.

[32] Ibid., 214.

[33] The transnational Islamic movement also made inroads into the Philippines through the JI. The JI is commonly viewed as a loose network of Southeast Asian Islamic militants founded by two Muslim preachers, Abdullah Achmad Sungkar and Abu Bakar Bashir. They recruited and taught small groups of Muslim scholars and students attracted to the Salafi and Wahhabi schools of Islam. The two soon gained adherents by preaching among radical Malaysian and Indonesian exiles, and by becoming actively involved in the recruitment of Muslims for the jihad in Afghanistan. Two of the their closest associates, Riduan Isamuddin (Hambali) and Mohammed Iqbal Rahman (Abu Jibril), fought in Afghanistan and were recruited by bin Ladin to establish a network of terrorist cells in Southeast Asia. The network emerged gradually in the 1980s in Indonesia from a militant group of Islamist scholars, students, and activists committed to spreading a stronger sense of Islamic identity throughout the region. In the 1990s, members of JI were further radicalized as they came into contact with other radical Muslim groups in Afghanistan and across Southeast Asia. JI's organizational development reached its apex in 1999-2000 through the Southeast Asian initiative set against the backdrop of personal connections between regional leaders and al-Qa'ida operatives in Afghanistan. Many intelligence and press reports tend to present JI as a creation of al-Qa'ida. However, although al-Qa'ida encouraged and assisted in the formation of JI, the latter is not a simple creation of bin Ladin, as it has its own regional agenda and is not considered a global terrorist network.

RSM's Ideology

RSM's jihadist ideology is largely influenced by Ahmet Santos' infatuation with Wahabbism, which also explains the group's affinity for al-Qa'ida's ideology. As is the case with ASG, it is possible to gain a view into RSM's beliefs by examining literature captured from the group. Based on documents seized in 2005, it seems that two works are particularly relevant to RSM's ideology: Shaykh Abdullah Azzam's *Defense of the Muslim Lands*, and *The Virtues of Shuhadah in the Path of Allah*, believed to be by the same author. The first document uses a question-and-answer approach to rationalizing jihad. The first part discusses the Great March of Islam in the contemporary period, a period in which "the woman leaves without the husband's permission and the son without his father's permission."[34] According to Azzam, the Great March is required in this period for the following purposes: 1) expanding the Islamic territory for the millions of Muslims; 2) saving the Umma; and 3) preventing the open areas of the world from becoming territories of the communists, Baptists, nationalists, and secularists.[35] The first

---

JI's long-term political objective is to create an Islamic state (*Daulah Islamiyh Nusantara*) composed of Malaysia, Indonesia, and Mindanao (and incorporating Singapore and Brunei). The core of JI is based in Indonesia, where it emerged around the "Ngruki school network" in Solo, Central Java. In 1985, Sungkar and Ba'syir fled to Malaysia and this marked the beginning of an extraordinary degree of organizing and networking building of what in 2002 would be called JI. JI experienced further expansion in Malaysia when Hambali and Jibril recruited Indonesian migrants and university lecturers and students at the University Tecknologi Malaysia. In August 2000, JI members, in cooperation with the MILF, tried to kill the Philippine ambassador to Indonesia in a car bomb attack in Jakarta. The Philippine cell was formed through Al-Ghozi who did liaison work with the MILF in the mid-1990s. In 2003, however, Al-Ghozi was killed in Central Mindanao by government forces after he escaped from a police detention center in Manila. His death and the ongoing MILF-Philippine government peace negotiations marked the decoupling of the MILF from JI as the former took a number of dramatic steps to distance itself further way from transnational terrorist organizations in an effort to forge a long-term and a comprehensive peace agreement with the Philippine government with the support of moderate Muslim countries and the West. See John Sidel, "Cracking Down in Indonesia," *Jakarta Post* (23 October 2002), 1, http://www.worldpress.org/article_model.cfm?article_model.cfm?id=938&dont=yes ; John Gershman, "Is Southeast Asia the Second Front?" *Foreign Affairs* 81, no. 4 (July/August 2002), 66; International Crisis Group Asia Briefing, *Al-Qaeda in Southeast Asia: The Case of the "Nguki Network" in Indonesia* (Jakarta/Brussels, 8 August 2002), 9; Paul A. Rodell, "Separatist Insurgency in the Southern Philippines," in *A Handbook of Terrorism and Insurgency in Southeast Asia*, ed. Andrew T. H. Tan (Cheltenham, UK; MA, USA: Edward Elgar Publications, 2007), 225-47.

[34] Shaykh Abdulah Azzam, *Defence of Muslim Land*, monograph version captured from the March 2005 Philippine National Police Operation against RSM in Quezon City, the Philippines, ch. 4.
[35] *Ibid*.

part of *Defense of the Muslim Lands* also denounces Muslims for waiting and weeping while Islamic regions fall under the control of the *kufr* and calls on all Muslims to follow Allah's command for the Great March that will liberate Palestine in one week and later Afghanistan.

The second portion of *Defense of the Muslim Lands* calls for waging a jihad despite the absence of an amir or caliphate that will lead this holy struggle. It urges the mujahidin to choose an amir among them and not to wait for the return of the caliphate that Azzam claims will never be restored. The third portion explains the reasons for a jihad in Afghanistan. Interestingly, the RSM members who copied this portion of Azzam's work overlooked the fact that the Soviet invasion of Afghanistan ended in 1989, and the current jihad in the country is now directed against the U.S. and the North Atlantic Treaty Organization (NATO). These NATO countries drove the Taliban regime from Kabul in 2001 and have since politically and militarily supported the secular regime of President Hamid Karzai. Yet, the RSM documents, seized in 2005, still state that the fighting in Afghanistan is for the defense of the Muslims against the aggression of the atheists (referring to the communists).[36] Similarly, the final sections of the document deal with the dilemma of fighting with Muslims who have shallow or superficial faith in Islam (referring to the Afghans in the 1980s) and with the Kaafirs (referring to the U.S. political and military support of the mujahidin in the 1970s and 1980s). This failure to update Azzam's work demonstrates an outright laziness and ideological passivity of RSM members. It is also reflective of the low level of understanding and creative theorizing about jihadist ideology among Islamist groups in the Philippines.

The second set of reading materials seized from RSM pertains to the *Virtues of a Shuhadah in the Path of Allah* culled primarily, again, from Azzam's work. The first part glorifies the Shaheed who has taken the path of Allah, that is, one who has taken part in a jihad. Jihad is defined as the struggle or fight against disbelievers with the sword until they accept Islam or pay the *jizya* (tax) by hand in a state of humiliation.[37] The document examines the glorious and blissful after-life of those who have shed their blood in a jihad, explaining that Allah has created a paradise of a hundred levels and the martyred mujahidin will be given the highest part of this paradise. They will also be allowed to roam around Paradise if they wish to do so. Furthermore, the document states that a Shaheed

---

[36] Ibid., 4.

[37] Author unknown, "Virtues of Shahadah in the Path of Allah: Adopted from the Works of Ash-Sheikh ash-Shaheed Abdullah Azzam," E:\My Web Pages\virtues-shuhadah. html.

will be granted seven special favors by Allah, namely: 1) forgiveness of sin; 2) a place in paradise; 3) a cloth of an iman (modest yet high quality); 4) marriage to seventy-two Hoor al-Ain (beautiful women of Paradise); 5) salvation from the grave; 6) protection from the great fear of Judgment Day; and 7) a crown of honor that will be placed on his head. At the same time, it asserts that those who are killed in a jihad will never experience any pain, except when they feel the prick of a needle. The document also expounds on the three types of martyrdom and argues that the best way to experience martyrdom is to die through hemorrhage when one's limbs are cut off by the sword during a jihad.[38] Promoting a transnational jihad, it affirms that "a military expedition in the sea is better than ten military expeditions on land."[39] Finally, it sanctifies the use of suicide tactics by mujahidin as it promises that martyrs who died by their own weapons will be amply rewarded with twice the amount of those killed by their enemies. It maintains that the Messenger (Muhammad) will bear witness that those who died with their own sword are martyrs in front of Allah. [40]

RSM's apparent reliance on *The Virtues of Shuhadah in the Path of Allah* confirms the fact that among the local Islamist groups in the Philippines, RSM is foremost in training its members to be "martyrs of Islamic faith" by becoming would-be-suicide bombers.[41] The group's use of this material is also indicative of its efforts to emulate al-Qa'ida's martyrdom operations as an offensive war against the *kufr*. Indeed, from Bin Ladin's point of view, the use of suicide or martyrdom constitutes the application of a radical and formidable instrument of violence in a new front of this particular episode of the long and protracted conflict between the transnational jihadist movement and the West.[42]

RSM's Tactics

With funding from ASG and JI, RSM has recruited Muslim converts, held terrorist trainings, and conducted initial terrorist operations in metropolitan Manila. RSM also sent some members to a MILF camp in Mindanao to undergo a Special Training Course prior to their deployment in Manila. RSM has since been held responsible for the following terrorist acts: 1) the March 2003 bombing of Davao International Airport in Mindanao; 2) the 27 February 2004 bombing M/V

---

[38] Ibid., 5.

[39] Ibid.

[40] Ibid., 8.

[41] Banlaoi (2007a), 214.

[42] Beverly Milton-Edwards, *Islamic Fundamentalism since 1945* (New York and Oxon: Routledge, 2005), 141.

Super Ferry 14 that killed 116 people and injured 300 passengers (with ASG's support); and 3) the 14 February 2005 simultaneous bombings (again in collaboration with ASG) in three Philippine cities—Makati City in Luzon, General Santos City, and Davao City in Mindanao.

Jihadist Ideology and Movement in the Philippines: Still in the Margins?

The presence of the aforementioned jihadist materials in ASG's and RSM's lairs suggests an ideological affinity with transnational Islamic fundamentalist groups that utilize sacred violence in their war against modernity, secularism, and the West. As explained above, the material studied by ASG and RSM were mostly derived from the works of Palestinian extremist Shaykh Abdullah Azzam, who, in turn, was influenced by the late Egyptian poet Sayyid Qutb. To Qutb, jihad should uproot the *Jahilli* (pagan or pre-Islamic) way of life and to replace it with Allah's sovereignty on earth (*Al-Hakimayyah*) through a vanguard (amir). The amir's basic task is to take the long journey leading to the realization of a Sharia-based society on earth.[43] Qutb argued that a jihad is not a defensive Islamic measure against the infidels; rather, jihad should be considered as a means of propagating the true character of Islam. The true Islamic nature, according to Qutb, could be actualized only through the proclamation of the freedom of man from servitude from other men, the establishment of the sovereignty of Allah throughout the world, the end of human arrogance and selfishness, and implementation of Divine Sharia rule over human affairs.[44]

These themes are clearly articulated in Abu Ramadan's *Jihad in the Philippines* and the documents seized from RSM. ASG's and RSM's materials also reflect Qutb's call for launching a jihad against three kinds of infidels: adversaries in wars; those who have concluded treaties with the faithful; and *Dhimmies*, or non-Muslims, residing in a Muslim state. Both ASG and RSM incorporate Qutb's notion of a continuing/offensive jihad to convert people to become true Muslims, ensure the Dhimmies' subjugation through their tax payments to an Islamic regime, and vanquish people who wage war against the Islamic world of Umma. At the same time, the literature seized from ASG and RSM clearly manifests these groups' acceptance of Qutb's argument that *jihad* should never be viewed as a defensive measure, but rather as an offensive device to keep the infidels at

---

[43] For an interesting work on the life and writings of Sayyid Qutb, see Adnan A. Mussalam, *From Secularism to Jihad: Sayyid Qutb and its Foundations of Radical Islamism* (Westport, CT: Praeger Publisher, 2005).

[44] Ibid., 161.

bay, and in the long run, to rid the earth of their corruption, materialism, and secularism.[45]

The two groups' reading material also suggests that ASG and RSM have adopted Azzam's romantic and idealized vision of jihad.[46] Indeed, the material strongly reflects Azzam's central idea that Islamic lands once ruled by Muslims that are now occupied by the infidels can only be liberated through a jihad. Moreover, according to this view, it is the obligation of every Muslim to participate in the holy struggle to restore Muslim sovereignty over these territories. Significantly, both ASG and RSM regard the entire pre-Hispanic Philippines as a Muslim territory. Thus, applying Azzam's ideology to the Philippines, jihad should not be confined to Mindanao, but should be waged all over the country.

Significantly, the ideological familiarity of ASG and RSM with the works of Qutb and Azzam is almost certainly a result of their links with al-Qa'ida, made possible by Janjalani's stint in Afghanistan in the late 1980s and ASG's ties with RSM in the early 21st century. Equally important, however, is the fact that the groups have simply focused on the works of Qutb and Azzam and seem to be generally oblivious to the works of more contemporary jihadist ideologues. Their ignorance indicates that the Abu Sayyaf and RSM are, in fact, marginal groups operating at the fringes of both transnational and domestic Islamic movements. Internationally, ASG is seen as a small cog in the transnational jihadist network; it originated in Afghanistan, but is not currently supported or guided by al-Qa'ida because of the former's propensity to engage in kidnapping and banditry.[47] The exposure of chief al-Qa'ida operatives in the aftermath of Yousef's foiled attempt to assassinate Pope John Paul II in 1995 led to the withdrawal of these key figures from the Philippines and the refocusing of the network attention from Mindanao to Malaysia.[48] In a way, links between al-Qa'ida and ASG (along with RSM) are comparable to the relationship between al-Qa'ida and the Hezbollah and other Palestinian terror groups; these groups do not conduct joint operational activity with al-Qa'ida despite some ad hoc

---

[45] Ibid., 182.

[46] In the words of Azzam: "Love of jihad has taken over my life, my soul, my sensation, my heart, and my emotion. If preparation for jihad is terrorism, then we are terrorists. If defending our honor is extremist, then we are extremists. If jihad against our enemies is fundamentalism, then we are fundamentalist." Ibid., 191.

[47] Milton-Edwards, 106.

[48] Abuza (2005), 42.

cooperation and personal or ideological relations.[49]

ASG and RSM are also marginal actors domestically. Contemporary mainstream Islamic resurgence in the Philippines is generally directed at the practice and teaching of classical or "high" Islam, not the militant or extremist brand of the faith.[50] Rather, it involves the building of more Arabic-style mosques, the use of muezzin chanting instead of a drum during the call for prayer, and the conversion of several Christians to Islam not only in Mindanao, but throughout the country. The mainstream movement also entails a return to Islamic fundamentals that do not require a participation in jihad. In other words, it denotes an intellectual and spiritual reflection of the faith's continuing relevance in the face of the dramatic and rapid socio-economic changes of the 21st century.[51] Such reflection requires: 1) the Muslims' mental preparation for reform or renewal; 2) formulation of a rationale and an intellectual basis for an Islamic reform and revival; and 3) transmission of this message (for reform or renewal) to the Umma for appropriate response. Politically, the mainstream Muslim movement led by the MILF is neither guided nor motivated by any jihadist ideology calling for a radical restructuring of Philippine society or an overthrow of the political system.[52] Instead, the MILF is a secessionist movement that pursues cultural, economic, and political self-determination to ensure the Filipino Muslims' control of their homeland in Mindanao. It is driven by one clear and simple ideology—ethno-nationalism, which has evolved from pure separatism into a desire to modify the nature of political and economic relationships between the Filipino Muslim and the Philippine state. The MILF aims to address the issue of landlessness for the majority of the Muslims in Mindanao and rectify misdirected state policies.[53] A noted American scholar specializing in the secessionist movement in Mindanao explains: "Muslim nationalists tend toward Islamic moderation not only because of the localized

---

[49] See Mathew Levitt, "Underlying the Terror Web: Identifying and Counter-acting the Phenomenon of Crossover between Terrorist Groups," *SAIS Review* 24, no. 1 (Winter 2004), 33.

[50] Robert Day McAmis, *Malay Muslim: The History and Challenge of Resurgent Islam in Southeast Asia* (Michigan/Cambridge: Wm. B. Fredman Publishing Co., 2002), 100.

[51] For an interesting work on the various forms of Islamic revival in the Philippines, see Mehol K. Sadain, *Global and Regional Trends in Islamic Resurgence: Their Implications on Southern Philippines* (Pasay City: Center for International Relations and Strategic Studies, 1994).

[52] See Thomas M. Mckenna, "Governing Muslims in the Philippines," *Harvard Asia-Pacific Review* 9, no. 1 (Winter 2007), 14.

[53] For a comprehensive discussion of the Mindanao problem, see Eric Gutierrez and Saturnino Borras, Jr., *The Moro Conflict: Landlessness and Misdirected State Policy* (Washington D.C: East-West Center, 2004).

nature of their political goals but also because they know that for their goals ultimately to succeed they must reach an accommodation with local Christians."[54]

Recently, the MILF has appeared restrained and sensible as it engages the Philippine government in a long and tedious peace negotiation to ensure its political control over a specific, geographically defined territory in Mindanao. To further accentuate its cautious and compromising stance, the MILF has denounced its links with the JI and ASG, cooperated with the Philippine government in tracking down Islamic extremists in Mindanao, and punished its own members who protect and shelter JI and ASG members wanted by the Philippine government and Western law-enforcement agencies.[55] Its leadership is likewise worried that a protracted or failed peace negotiation between the MILF and the government will only promote conditions that foster terrorism and Islamic fundamentalism.[56] Consequently, the present MILF leaders have focused on forging a peace deal with the Philippine government and currying political and economic favor from moderate Muslim countries in Southeast Asia, the U.S., and the European Union. Thus, the MILF is not inclined to solidify or revive its earlier links with al-Qa'ida, which would jeopardize its working relationship with the West and moderate Muslim regimes in Southeast Asia.[57] These developments, in turn, have marginalized Islamic jihadist groups like ASG and RSM.

At the same time, ASG's illegal activity, particularly its kidnap-for-ransom activities, has led to its perception as a criminal group, rather than a militant Islamic organization.[58] Indeed, one American counter-terrorism expert, Zachary Abuza, has argued that the group is above all a criminal nuisance with no apparent link to international terrorist organizations.[59] In Abuza's opinion, the Abu Sayyaff is dangerous to the Philippine government not because it is a

---

[54] Mckenna, 19.

[55] Ibid., 14.

[56] See Rodell (2007), 242.

[57] See Paul A. Rodell, "The Philippines and the Challenge of International Terrorism," in *Terrorism and Violence in Southeast Asia: Transnational Challenges and Regional Stability*, ed. Paul J. Smith (New York: M.E. Sharpe, Inc., 2005), 138.

[58] Andrew T.H. Tan, *Southeast Asia: Threats in the Security Environment* (Singapore: Marshall Cavendish Academic, 2006), 165. See also James Hookway, "Terrorist Cells Band Together in Philippines, Officials Say Death of Abu Sayyaf Leader Doesn't Mark Victory," *The Wall Street Journal Asia* (22 January 2007), 11.

[59] Abuza (2003), 111.

militant Islamic group, but rather as a "criminal organization that threatens law and order and development."[60] In *Seeds of Terror*, noted journalist Maria Ressa alleges that ASG has been corrupted into a shakedown operation, albeit one with links with al-Qa'ida and with ambitions to carry out terrorist acts for monetary reasons.[61] The Philippine military apparently shares this viewpoint, stating that the group's members are "plain bandits that make money [through] kidnap-for-ransom activities."[62]

Finally, ASG and RSM have also suffered from, and are likely to continue to suffer from, counter-terrorism efforts. Of particular importance to these efforts is the comprehensive plan concluded in 2006 between the Philippines and the United States for joint security exercises in the Philippines,[63] which include activities in Central Mindanao, regarded by the Pacific Command as "a window of terrorism not only in the Philippines but also in the entire Southeast Asia region."[64] Operations involve the crucial and tactical deployment of American reconnaissance planes that track ASG's movements in the thick tropical jungle of Sulu and the periodic conduct of humanitarian operations to wean away Muslim villages from these Islamic militants. These operations have resulted to some tactical success against ASG; American military support and assistance enabled the AFP to form and upgrade a tactical maneuver unit (Task Force Comet) that has restricted ASG's freedom of movement and minimized the group's capability to conduct terrorist operations in other parts of Mindanao. More significantly, Philippine troops neutralized Abu Sayyaff head Khadaffy Janjalani in September 2006, and his presumed successor, Abu Sulaiman, in January 2007 with the help of American tactical intelligence.[65] The neutralizations of these key ASG leaders created a leadership and ideological vacuum within the group, and resulted in the emergence of various factions, each with its own separate agenda and

---

[60] Rodell, 113.

[61] Maria A. Ressa, *Seeds of Terror: an Eye Witness Account of Al-Qaeda's Newest Center of Operations in Southeast Asia* (New York, NY: Simon and Schuster, 2003), 124.

[62] "Abu Sayyaff Reduced to Plain Bandits," *The Filipino Express* 22, no. 26 (27 June – 3 July 2008), 18. See also "AFP; Abu Sayyaf Largely Degraded but Stull a Threat in Mindanao," *The Filipino Express* 22, no. 28, (11 July – 17 July 2008), 1, 28.

[63] Jose T. Barbieto, "R.P.-U.S. Military Exercise," *Business World* (4 February 2005). p.1. http://proquest.umi.com/pqdweb?did=789060131&sid=2&Fmit=3&clientld=47883&RQT=309&VName=PQD

[64] Jaime Laude, "R.P.-U.S. War Games Set in Cotabato," *The Philippine Star* (14 January 2006), 1, 8.

[65] "U.S. Troops on Mission of Love and Stealth in RP," *The Filipino Express* 21, no. 11 (12 March – 18 March 2007), 16.

motivation.[66] Moreover, without a central leader or amir, ASG's ideological and religious motivation diminished, replaced by pure and simple greed.[67]

Meanwhile, in March 2005, the Philippine National Police raided RSM headquarters in Quezon City, thwarting a terrorist plot during the Holy Week and leading to the arrest of key RSM members. This breakthrough has since substantially weakened RSM as an Islamic extremist group.[68]

Conclusion

An analysis of reading materials seized from ASG and RSM provide strong evidence of these groups' affinity with transnational jihadist ideologies. Given ASG's earlier ties with al-Qa'ida and later with RSM, it is not surprising that the materials captured from the groups were mostly culled from or inspired by the works of Azzam and, by implication, Qutb; however, both groups have crudely and mechanically adopted the ideas of these two jihadist ideologues without subjecting their beliefs to critical analysis or any creative modifications. Evidently, they are not familiar with the more recent works of contemporary jihadist ideologues from the Middle East, North America, and Southeast Asia, which implies that ASG and RSG are marginalized groups operating at the fringes of both international and domestic Islamic movements. Internationally, these two groups have lost their earlier connections with al-Qa'ida because of ASG's bandit-like behavior and bin Ladin's decision to shift his organization's focus and efforts from the Philippines to other parts of Southeast Asia as a matter of tactical exigency. Domestically, the two jihadist groups have failed to influence the larger and more popular secessionist movement, the MILF, which is still primarily motivated and guided by ethno-nationalism rather than a jihadist ideology as it negotiates a peace agreement with the Philippine government. ASG's involvement in criminal activities and banditry by the late 1990s has raised further doubts about its credibility as a jihadi group. Moreover, U.S. military assistance to the AFP has resulted in the neutralization of its leaders and potential ideologues. Overall, the study of ASG and RSM lends credence to Professor Hussin Mutalib's observation that:

> Misperception abounds concerning radical Islam in Southeast Asia. Political Islam in this region is neither new nor necessarily related

---

[66] "AFP; Abu Sayyaf Largely Degraded but Stull a Threat in Mindanao," 28.
[67] Ibid.
[68] See Banlaoi (2007b).

to terrorism. Islamists were at the forefront of the independence struggle in both Indonesia and Malaysia, and terrorism is not unique to the extremists of the Muslim faith. Not only is militant Islam in Southeast Asia scattered, but it is also confined to small and marginalized groups...[69]

---

[69] Hussin Mutalib, "Misunderstood: Political Islam in Southeast Asia," *Harvard International Review* 28, no. 2 (Summer 2006), 84.

Ideology, Religion, and Mobilization in the Southern Thai Conflict

Joseph Chinyong Liow

Introduction

Since 2004, violence has become a regular occurrence along Thailand's southern border. A rejuvenated separatist movement, the BRN-Coordinate (Barison Revolusi National-Coordinate or National Revolutionary Front-Coordinate) is believed to have sparked the recent wave of violence on 4 January with a raid on a military camp; following the BRN assault, bombings, targeted killings, arson and attacks on military convoys has become commonplace. Indeed, violence in the provinces of Pattani, Yala, and Narathiwat has accounted for more than 3,000 deaths to date, and shows no signs of abating. Although the conflict is relatively low intensity in nature, the ongoing violence deserves attention, particularly for the absence of any claim of responsibility by its perpetrators. Moreover, while analysts and observers mostly agree that the BRN-Coordinate has emerged as a major actor in the violence, some have argued that several newer groups may have surfaced and are playing a major part in the conflict.[1]

Another ambiguous feature of the conflict in southern Thailand is the relative dearth of information regarding the key ideological drivers of the fighting. Unlike their counterparts in other regional clashes, including separatists in Aceh, Irian Jaya (or West Papua), and Mindanao, as well as religiously-inspired extremists such as members of Jemaah Islamiyah, insurgents in southern Thailand have not articulated the ideological underpinnings of their groups' violence. Based on present evidence, the southern Thai conflict does not appear to coalesce around the vitriolic religious ideology of an Abu Bakar Bashir, a religio-political blueprint such as that mapped out by the late Salamat Hashim and currently being set in motion by the MILF in the southern Philippines, or a coherent separatist agenda similar to the *Gerakan Aceh Merdeka* (Aceh Freedom Movement) struggle. Given this absence of a clear ideological leader or platform, any serious attempt to uncover the impetus to the southern Thailand conflict would predictably be an arduous task, compounded further by the murky nature

---

[1] According to a range of reports, some of these groups include Hikmatullah Abadan, RKK (Runda Kumpulan Kecil), Pemuda, Thai United Southern Underground, and most recently, the Mujahidin Shura Council of Southeast Asia and Patani Malay Consultative Congress. A useful typology of the degree of organization and institutionalization of the ongoing insurgency is provided by Duncan McCargo. See Duncan McCargo, *Tearing the Land Apart: Islam and Legitimacy in Southern Thailand* (Ithaca, N.Y.: Cornell University Press, 2008), 168-74.

of the conflict and the mystery surrounding the identity of the perpetrators.

Given that caveat, the limited amount of material available in the form of booklets and pamphlets detailing to varying degrees the motivations of some actors can be supplemented with interviews of insurgents from both the previous generation of separatist fighters and those involved in the current conflict. The combination of these sources can provide a fairly cogent map of some ideological pillars of the ongoing insurgency. Indeed, paucity of material notwithstanding, it is increasingly urgent that careful, considered analysis of the underlying motivating factors to the conflict be undertaken. This is especially true when considering the Thai state's visible inability to make structural and sustainable headway in counter-insurgency operations.[2] It is with this process in mind that this chapter attempts a preliminary mapping exercise by analysing jihadi ideas and texts that have surfaced in southern Thailand, investigating the ideological underpinnings of indoctrination and recruitment in the insurgency, and assessing the overall religious character of the ongoing conflict in Thailand's southern Muslim-majority provinces. The chapter posits two arguments: first, while there have been attempts among the insurgents to reference religious ideas, for the most part these are local in nature, centring on local ideas and vehicles of transmission; second, while religious metaphors and jihadi ideas are salient features to meta-narratives depicting the violence in southern Thailand as a "religious conflict," this should not distract from the highly-localised ethno-nationalist and political objectives that lie at its heart.

History from the Patani Perspective

In many respects, what we witness today in southern Thailand is but the latest manifestation of latent, longstanding tension between the Bangkok-based central government and a once fiercely independent Malay-Islamic sultanate that was brought under Siamese control through a mixture of coercion as well as political and diplomatic machinations. Simply put, it is the struggle for self-determination along ethno-cultural lines that remains at the heart of the problem in the southern border provinces.

The population of southern Thailand is predominantly ethnic Malay-Muslim, thereby differentiating it from the rest of the country. Historically, the provinces—once collectively known as Patani Darussalam—enjoyed various

---

[2] The degree of success is debateable, and the Thai government has attempted to enact programs favorable to the Malay-Muslim community.

degrees of autonomy despite being forcefully incorporated into the sphere of influence of Siamese suzerainty in 1786. On several occasions, leaders of Patani refused to send required tribute, leading to Siamese recriminations that resulted in wars between Siam and Patani, which for the latter entered into local folklore as wars of resistance.[3] This historical legacy is kept alive through oral and local print history, representative of the tension and mutual distrust between the central state in Bangkok and the provinces in the south.

Such historical and geopolitical considerations have been further aggravated by Bangkok's repeated disregard for local culture, religious identity, and practices in its administration of the southern provinces. One major point of contention has been the central government's reluctance to accord Malay language the status and legitimacy desired by local communities; another has been the disconnect between Thai and Malay perceptions of the role and relevance of Islamic education. For the Malay community of the southern provinces, Islamic schools have long been seen as a major social and cultural institution, not merely a repository of religious knowledge. Moreover, it is in the *pondok* (lit. hut) Islamic schools, ubiquitous institutions since the late 19th century, that local narratives of Patani history have been perpetuated and Malay language (in the form of the Jawi traditional Malay script and the Patani Malay dialect) kept alive. By contrast, the Thai establishment viewed Islamic schools with great suspicion. Given their emphasis on religious knowledge, these schools are not perceived to provide the necessary training required to support the building of a modern Thai nation-state. More importantly, these schools have been viewed as progenitors of contrarian views on Thai history, meaning that their staff's loyalty to the Thai state has been questioned. Finally, Islamic schools have been suspected to be key recruitment and indoctrination grounds for the Malay-based separatist movements. These differences have been amplified by the fact that there is an intimate correlation between Malay ethnicity and the Islamic religion, to the extent that Jawi, and not Arabic, is considered the "language of Islam" in the region. In other words, various policies enacted by the Thai government over the years to curb Malay cultural and religious expression have contributed to a mood of resistance against the state.

Resistance to the central state peaked in the 1960s with the formation of organized armed separatist groups. Among the most prominent were the *Barisan Revolusi Nasional*, formed in 1963, and PULO (Pattani United Liberation

---

[3] Surin Pitsuwan, *Islam and Malay Nationalism: A Case Study of the Malay-Muslims of Southern Thailand* (Bangkok: Thai Khadi Research Institute, 1985), 33.

Organization), formed in 1968. Notably, the founding leaders of these two groups were both Islamic religious teachers. Groups such as BNPP (*Barisan Nasional Pembebasan Patani* or National Liberation Front of Patani) and GMIP (*Gerakan Mujahideen Islam Pattani* or the Mujahideen Movement of Patani) would later emerge as the separatist movement expanded. An attempt in the 1990s to form an umbrella organization to bring these disparate groups together through the formation of *Bersatu* (also known in some sources as the United Front for the Liberation of Patani) failed from the outset, a victim of factionalism and competition both across its constituent groups as well as within them.[4]

While there are clearly continuities between previous epochs of resistance and the contemporary insurgency, it is the differences that have proven most striking. Tactically, the current generation of insurgents have been considerably more brutal and indiscriminate than their predecessors. Contemporary groups have been known to select targets where there is a high risk of "collateral damage" to civilian lives and infrastructure. Furthermore, the insurgency itself has transformed from a rural-based guerrilla struggle to an urban resistance movement; in cities, insurgents can melt easily into the population, thereby making intelligence gathering much more difficult.

The Importance of Determining the Role of Religion in the Southern Thai Insurgency

Given the murky nature of the conflict in southern Thailand, absence of any claims of responsibility on the part of its perpetrators, and lack of clearly articulated objectives and goals, scholars and analysts continue to debate the key ideological drivers underpinning the southern insurgency. Against the backdrop of the emerging transnational threat of al-Qa'ida and the corresponding American-led "global war on terror," uncertainty about the religious dimensions to the conflict in the Muslim-majority provinces of southern Thailand has garnered increasing interest.

Fixation with the religious dimension to the southern Thai conflict stems, in large part, from the fact that the chief avenue of recruitment for the current insurgency is widely believed to be Islamic religious schools.[5] For instance, in April 2007,

---

[4] For more information about the separatist movements active in southern Thailand, see International Crisis Group, "Southern Thailand: Insurgency, Not Jihad," *International Crisis Group*, Asia Report no. 98 (18 May 2005).

[5] In recent times, it seems that, beyond Islamic schools, recruitment venues have included teashops and village-based social events.

General Wattanachai Chaaimuanwong, then chief security advisor to Prime Minister Surayud Chulanont, declared that it was likely the new generation of militants are "loosely guided by a large council" of veteran fighters and religious leaders.[6] Furthermore, insurgents occasionally appropriate religious epithets to justify their struggle, the most common being the depiction of themselves as "mujahidin" carrying out a "jihad," or holy warriors carrying out a holy struggle. Another common refrain is that Islam justifies an "uprising against unjust rule."[7] Finally, religious motifs related to notions of religious governance and lifestyle have been regularly mobilized in the course of conflict, where the "jihad" in southern Thailand is portrayed as a war to drive out Siamese "*kafir*" and reinstate Muslim governance.

Not surprisingly, the Thai security establishment has been particularly perturbed by the seemingly religious flavour of the conflict in the south. Cognizant of global trends, policy-makers in Bangkok are quick to point to growing Islamic religiosity across the Muslim world that quickly translates into acts of defiance. In the case of southern Thailand, Thai veterans of the mujahidin struggle against the Soviet Union in Afghanistan in the 1980s serve as a source of inspiration to the current conflict.[8] This generates a contradictory message whereby political leaders and security officials are reluctant to publicly admit the role of returnees as inspirational leaders returning to the fray, while also pointing to the risks of increasing religiosity.

At first glance, it seems logical that insurgents' use of religious references, such as the Qur'anic injunction to fight against the oppression of Muslims and talk about liberating their Patani Darussalam homeland from Siamese colonialism, resonate with the plight of the Malay-Muslims in southern Thailand. It is thus tempting for analysts to conclude that these insurgents are in fact fighting for Islam and thereby susceptible to the lures of the global jihad and foreign extremist ideologies. To that end, some have tenuously attempted to connect the dots between the Thai conflict and rising Islamic consciousness and the growth of Islamism on the part of Malay-Muslims in southern Thailand, implying a risk of greater violence. These analysts reach such conclusions, however, without

---

[6] Interview with General Wattanachai, Bangkok, 22 April 2007.

[7] Interviews conducted with a member of the original BRN, who is now a member of BRN-C, and who is currently in charge of several cells involved in the contemporary insurgency and on condition of anonymity, in May 2006, February 2008, and March 2009 (I am not at liberty to publicly disclose the venue of these meetings).

[8] "Government seeks help from local clerics," *The Nation*, 4 June 2004.

ever demonstrating how and why a pious Malay-Muslim takes the gargantuan leap to militancy and violence. At the same time, those who link the Thai conflict to Islamism fail to explain why the conflict has remained contained in southern border provinces, or why the Malay-Muslims of southern Thailand—both insurgents and common folk—have refused to acknowledge the mediating roles that their non-Malay co-religionists elsewhere in Thailand have offered to play.

This is not to say that religion does not play a role in the conflict – religious dogma cannot be detached from ethno-cultural references. Rather, religion animates the narrative of Malay ethno-nationalism, injecting further meaning and intelligibility into the drive for self-determination. The next section of this chapter analyses the role that religion plays in the southern Thailand conflict.

Attempting to Measure the Actual Impact of Religion on the Southern Thai Conflict

Islamic Schools and Scholars

As noted above, the central Thai government suspects that Islamic schools in the southern provinces are key vehicles for the indoctrination and recruitment of new insurgents. To a certain extent, such concerns are well earned. For instance, young men who attended a weekend Islamic school recalled in a 2006 interview how an *uztaz* (Islamic religious teacher) spoke passionately about the moral obligation of the "*anak Patani*" (children of Patani) to take back Patani from the *kafir* Siamese.[9] This *ustaz* further demanded unquestionable loyalty to the cause of the liberation of Patani from the occupying forces.[10] Nevertheless, evidence suggests that most recruitment in religious schools is a highly decentralized process involving small, unofficial study groups.[11] As a recent study of southern Thailand conducted by the International Crisis Group explains:

> Recruitment agents, often religious teachers, reportedly select
> youths who display three key characteristics: piety,
> impressionability, and agility. Agents recruit these youths into
> small groups, initially by befriending and inviting them to join
> discussion or prayer groups. Candidates are sounded out in
> conversations about Patani history. Those who seem receptive to

---

[9] "Alone in the Shadow of Militants," *The Nation*, 21 May 2006.
[10] Ibid.
[11] Interview with Thai Special Branch, Bangkok, 13 July 2005.

liberationist ideology are invited to join the movement.[12]

It is important to note, however, that the impact of Islamic schools on the Thai insurgency seems to come not from the use of "Islamic studies" to indoctrinate and recruit extremists, but rather through the dissemination of local histories, in particular narratives of oppression and colonization. Indeed, according to insurgents, the role of religious functionaries does not extend to tactical and strategic matters.[13]

Looking at religious scholars more broadly, there is a real division as to whether the conflict in southern Thailand may be properly framed as a "jihad." While classical Muslim scholars stress that jihad can be expressed in many forms, the concept itself has taken on a threatening note by virtue of the fact that Muslim militants are using only one aspect of jihad—that which calls for armed struggle against oppressive and hostile enemies of Islam—to sanction and legitimize their actions.

One of the primary proponents of the view that the Thai conflict *cannot* be properly described as a jihad is Ismail Lutfi, the respected Salafi cleric accused by some of being the Wahhabi leader of Jemaah Islamiyah in Thailand. According to Lufti, describing the ongoing conflict in southern Thailand as a religious struggle betrays "a very general and simplistic understanding of *jihad*."[14] In the literature that he has produced, Lutfi echoes classic Islamic thought by stressing that only a recognized religious authority (*pemimpin agung bagi ummat Islam*) can declare jihad, and even then it can only be declared after other avenues of *dakwah* (proselytisation) have been exhausted.[15] He further instructs that "Islam forbids the spilling of Muslim blood," a view that takes on greater currency in the context of ongoing violence in southern Thailand, which has increasingly witnessed the killing of fellow Muslims (including students of Islamic schools) by militants.[16] Members of the *Jemaat Tabligh* proselytisation movement,

---

12 International Crisis Group, 26.

13 During an anti-government protest at Sungai Padi district, a known hotbed of the insurgency, religious teachers were seen providing refreshment for the women and children protesters. Interviews conducted with a member of the original BRN, and who is currently in charge of several cells involved in the contemporary insurgency and on condition of anonymity, in May 2006 (he also instructed that were not to divulge where the meeting took place).

14 Interview with Ismail Lutfi, Pattani, 14 January 2006.

15 Ismail Lutfi Japakiya, *Islam: Agama Penjana Kedamaian Sejagat* (Alor Star, Kedah: Pustaka Darussalam, 2005), 76.

16 Ibid., 81.

meanwhile, claim that the conditions for armed jihad have not been met in southern Thailand because Islam has not been banned, and hence the spread of Islam should be done via peaceful means.[17]

Such benign views are counterbalanced by more malignant perspectives on jihad and violence in southern Thailand that have also appeared on the discursive landscape. An *ustaz* with known links to PULO, in the course of an interview, said that *jihad qital* (armed jihad) had long been necessary in southern Thailand because of the victimization of the Malay people by the oppressive Thai state.[18] This *ustaz* felt that offensive jihad was necessary to ensure the freedom not just of religion, but of Malay identity, in the southern provinces.

Echoing a similar perspective, an *ustaz* with links to GMIP averred that the time for *jihad qital* had descended upon the *"tiga wilayah"* (three provinces, referring to the local nomenclature for the Malay-Muslim provinces of Narathiwat, Pattani, and Yala).[19] This *ustaz* was especially critical of Ismail Lutfi's views regarding the appropriateness of jihad in southern Thailand. He suggests that these views stem from Lufti's "Saudi-oriented" perspective, which focuses on developments in Islamic thought during the religion's expansive phase of the Prophet in Mecca (*"zaman nabi di Makkah"*), when the message focused on the spread of Islam peacefully (*"menyebarkan shari'a Islam dengan cara damai"*). The *ustaz* took issue with this perspective because, in his view, the conditions being encountered by Thai Muslims today are similar to those which confronted the Prophet during the Medinan era (*"zaman nabi di Madina"*). He defines this era as the "assault and violation of Muslim lands by non-Muslims (*orang yang mencerobuhi bumi kita*)" from polytheistic Mecca. Under these conditions, *jihad qital* is not only warranted; it is necessary.

Yet another religious teacher claimed that if he discovered that his students were active in militancy against the Thai state, he would not stop them because they would be engaging in a "legitimate struggle" that is several centuries old. When asked about Siamese aid and assistance to Patani, he reportedly responded: "Do you know how humiliating it is for the Malays to seek assistance from Siam?"[20]

---

[17] Interview at Markaz Dakwah Yala, Yala, 14 January 2006. This *ustaz* however was not specific as to what he meant by the "conditions" for *jihad qital*.

[18] *Ustaz* interview, Pattani, 8 May 2006.

[19] *Ustaz* interview, Pattani, 10 May 2006.

[20] This anecdote was shared by Don Pathan during a seminar at the Rajaratnam School of International Studies, Singapore, 9 July 2007.

Interestingly, even when the notion of jihad is supported, the use of religion and theology to sanction acts of violence does not stem from established theological literature, or judicial decree, or sophisticated Qur'anic exegesis, but rather from the oral instruction that religious teachers provide to their students. This supports the notion that, unlike the situation in the southern Philippines or Indonesia, the conflict in southern Thailand does not draw from the teachings and writings of prominent clerics; there is no equivalent of an Abu Bakar Bashir or Hashim Selamat, to say nothing of a Abu Muhammad al-Maqdisi or Abu Hamza al-Masri.

Jihadi Literature

Despite the lack of any prominent ideologue, at least two pieces of literature have been produced in the Jawi language that may be classified as "jihadist texts." Each is worthy of detailed review.

- *Jihad Fi Sabillillah Pengertian dan Bidang* (The Understanding and Call for Struggle in the Way of Allah)[21]

The first of the jihadist pieces of literature available to insurgents in southern Thailand is *Jihad Fi Sabillillah Pengertian dan Bidang*. It is an undated booklet, written by someone called Hassan Nikmatullah. Obtained by the author from a rural Islamic school in Pattani province, the booklet is an exegesis on the concept of jihad, but it quickly becomes evident that Nikmatullah's primary goal is to extol the virtues of offensive jihad.

The booklet begins by establishing two examples of the understanding of *jihad fi sabillilah*.[22] Using Qur'anic verses, Nikmatullah argues that jihad can be defined either in terms of the performance of rituals such as prayers and fasting, or as the call to wage war against infidels (*kafir*).[23] He further suggests that Muslims have "failed to comprehend the true meaning of *jihad*," blaming this failure on the *ulama*.[24] Echoing a riposte that is characteristic of Salafi criticisms of traditional religious leaders, the author suggests that the *ulama* tends to subscribe only to

---

[21] The following discussion is taken from Joseph Chinyong Liow, *Islam, Education, and Reform in Southern Thailand: Tradition and Transformation* (Singapore: Institute of Southeast Asian Studies, 2009).

[22] See immediately below for a clarification of *jihad fi sabillilah*.

[23] Hassan Hikmatullah, *Jihad Fi Sabililllah Pengertian dan Bidang* [The Understanding and Call for Struggle in the Way of Allah], Undated, 4.

[24] Ibid., 5.

meanings of jihad advocated by classical Islamic scholars; it is this rigid and hardened position on jihad that accounts for the community's inability to fully appreciate the concept. Nikmatullah proceeds to define *jihad fi sabilillah* as "striving for something with one's strength and for the sake of mankind, and without care for anything except for God's blessings."[25] He later argues that jihad conducted in this manner "is the most important positive deed in the eyes of Allah."[26]

Nikmatullah provides three conditions for the practice of *jihad fi sabilillah*: (1) performing *amal* (action in the name of Islam) to the best of one's abilities, (2) performing *amal* sincerely for Allah, and (3) performing *amal* in accordance to the *sunnah* of the Prophet.[27] He then proceeds to expand on these three practices by making extensive references to the Qur'an and numerous *hadith*.[28] Next, the author elaborates on the advantages of *jihad fi sabilillah*, dividing it into two categories: its advantages in the current life, and its advantages in the afterlife. In the former case, Nikmatullah explains that the advantage of jihad in the current life lies in the fact that its conduct will be guided by God and will return in the form of blessings to the believer.[29] Specifically, a person who performs jihad will obtain "war gains (bounty)" and will be widely respected, particularly if he triumphs over the *kafir*.[30] In the latter case, a person who wages jihad will be ensured a place in heaven and enjoy its benefits. Moreover, the person who conducts jihad will have all his sins forgiven.[31]

From here, Nikmatullah progresses to a discussion on the categories of jihad. He classifies jihad in four categories, namely, (1) jihad at a personal level, (2) jihad at a societal level, (3) jihad at an economic level, and (4) jihad at a political level. Citing a *surah* from the Qur'an that relates the encounter between Moses and the Pharaoh in which Moses challenges the Pharaoh's claims that he is god, Nikmatullah argues that the best form of jihad is one which is conducted in order to uphold justice for the betterment of one's country.[32] To justify his emphasis on armed jihad, the author quotes from the Qur'an (Al-Tahrim 9), where it is written "Oh prophet of God, wage jihad against *kafir* and *munafikin* [hypocrites] and

---

[25] Ibid., 9.
[26] Ibid., 38.
[27] Ibid., 10.
[28] Ibid., 11-32.
[29] Ibid., 34-35.
[30] Ibid., 36.
[31] Ibid., 39.
[32] Ibid., 44.

ensure that you deal with them in a tough manner as they are inhibitors of hell and hell is the worst place one can live in."[33] From this verse, he suggests that there are two targets of jihad: jihad against *kafir* and jihad against *munafikin*. Nikmatullah further references a *hadith* from Imam Muslim in which the Prophet is quoted as saying:

> There are no prophets that were sent before me to an *ummah* but to stop from doing deeds prevented by God and to ask of them to perform deeds required by God of them. Those among the people who jihad to stop an illegal act using their hands are among the *mukmin* [people blessed by God]. Those among the people who jihad to stop an illegal act using their tongue are among the *mukmin* and those among the people who jihad to stop an illegal act using their heart are among the *mukmin* but this is the weakest form of *iman* [faith].[34]

Nikmatullah deduces from this *hadith* that the Prophet was exhorting Muslims to conduct armed jihad in order to ensure peace and "extinguish the fire of anarchy" that arises from the injustice of the government. Having affirmed the centrality of "jihad of the hand," Nikmatullah proceeds to cite other examples of jihad, which include being good to one's parents, supporting widows, loyalty to and taking care of spouses and their property, and personal jihad through prayer and fasting.[35] Considering the lack of attention he gives to these practices, which is discernibly less compared to his exposition on armed jihad, they are clearly of secondary importance to his mind.

The booklet *Jihad Fi Sabillillah Pengertian dan Bidang* has two distinguishable traits. First, it is clearly Salafist in orientation, given its author's direct criticism of the traditionalist *ulama* for "misleading" the Muslim community. Second, despite Nikmatullah's attempts to elucidate the various natures of jihad, it is clear from the flow of the text that he privileges *jihad qital* or armed jihad. The Salafist-jihadist emphasis in this book contravenes not just the perspectives of more moderate Salafi-reformists like Ismail Lutfi, but also popular Sufi readings of jihad, which maintain that jihad should "originate from the heart, not the hand."[36] Moreover, despite the book's strong focus on armed jihad, Nikmatullah

---

[33] Ibid., 45.
[34] Ibid., 46.
[35] Ibid., 47-53.
[36] *Ustaz* interview, Pattani, 13 January 2006.

fails to mention any of the guidelines or codes of conduct developed under classical Islamic thinking for the regulation of armed jihad. For instance, there is no attempt to distinguish between *jihad* as *fard 'kifaya* (referring to the offensive jihad, which only some Muslims need to undertake) and as *fard 'ayn* (which refers to the defensive jihad all Muslims are obliged to undertake in their own way). Nor does the author feel any need to highlight one of the most controversial and well-concealed features of the ethics and law regarding jihad, namely, the fact that in the Qur'an (22:40), it is intimated that Islam permits Muslims to carry arms to defend those who are oppressed and persecuted *regardless* of race or religion.[37]

Nikmatullah also fails to explain the legalistic and regulatory terms of jihad, particularly the centrality of the *imam* in the call to arms. In classical Islamic thought, *jihad qital* can only be undertaken upon the sanction of the imam or *mujtahid*, who concurrently serves both as the legitimizing ideologue as well as the "commander-in-chief." The fact that *jihad qital* cannot be launched without the issuance of prior notice through three warnings, or that there are legitimate and illegitimate targets of armed jihad (civilians or those not trained in weapons, for example, are not to be targeted), have also been overlooked. Nor does the book discuss the terms for the termination of jihad in accordance to the Prophet's injunction that reads: "fight until oppression ends and God's laws prevail. But if [the enemy] desists, then you must also cease hostilities."[38] Finally, discussion on the societal aspects of *jihad qital*, particularly the fact that parental approval is required for offensive jihad of *fard 'kifaya*, or even that under certain circumstances non-Muslims can be enlisted for jihad (even if he is of the same religion as the enemy), are avoided.

- *Berjihad di Pattani* (The Conduct of a Holy Struggle in Pattani)[39]

The second piece of jihadist literature relevant to the conflict in southern Thailand was discovered following the 28 April 2004 series of coordinated attacks conducted by militants across Pattani, Yala, and Songkhla, which culminated in the massacre of thirty-two militants and one civilian at the historical Krisek (Krue Se) mosque. According to reports, security officials

---

[37] See Muhammad Haniff Hassan and Mohamed bin Ali, *Questions and Answers on Jihad* (Singapore: The Islamic Religious Council of Singapore (MUIS), 2007), 6.

[38] Al-Qur'an 2:193.

[39] See Joseph Chinyong Liow, "Muslim Resistance in Southern Thailand and Southern Philippines: Religion, Ideology, and Politics," *Policy Studies* 24 (Washington D.C.: East-West Center Washington, 2006).

uncovered a controversial manuscript entitled *Berjihad di Pattani*, written in local Jawi script, on the bodies of several of the dead militants in Krisek. The text is also believed to have been circulated in a number of Islamic schools in the southern provinces, becoming not only part of their curriculum but of the resistance narrative as well.

Berjihad di Pattani, allegedly penned in the obscure town in Kelantan (northern Malaysia), calls for a holy war of liberation to free the kingdom of Patani from "colonialists."[40] Liberally peppered with metaphorical references and verses from the Qur'an, *Berjihad* reflects in its polemics the familiar radical Islamist diatribe that conjures a Manichean world struggle between Islam and the *Jahiliyyah*.[41] That notwithstanding, what stands out about *Berjihad* is the objectives to which Islamic idioms are directed: mobilization of the population to support and sacrifice for the reinstatement of Patani Darussalam. To that effect, the author presses the following:

> We should be ashamed of ourselves for sitting idly and doing nothing while the colonialists trampled our brothers and sisters. The wealth that belongs to us has been seized. Our rights and freedom have been curbed, and our religion and culture have been sullied.... Our late parents, brothers, and sisters sacrificed their lives for their land as warriors; they left behind a generation with warrior blood flowing in their veins. Today, let us make a call, so that the warrior blood will flow again and the generation will emerge again.[42]

The author proceeds to extol martyrdom, which emerges as a central theme in the book. He writes: "*Wira Shuhada* [martyrs], how glorious we will be if we fall as warriors of our land.... When Martyrs are killed, they are not dead but alive next to God... [and] will watch and listen to every piece of news to see if their children will follow in their footsteps."[43] Another striking feature of the polemics in *Berjihad* is the writer's attack not only on "colonialists" as *Jahili* (people of the ignorance), but certain Muslims as well. For instance, he suggests that while some Muslims may be performing the Five Pillars of the faith, "their actions or

---

[40] The author of *Berjihad di Pattani* is believed to be a Kelantan native who has gone by the aliases of Poh Su, Poh Su Ismail, and Ismail Jaafar.

[41] *Berjihad Di Pattani*, author's personal copy, 10 August 2002, 2.

[42] Ibid., 5.

[43] Ibid. The author cites *Al-I-Imran* 3: 169 to substantiate this call, and *Hadith Shaheeh Muslim*, book 1, 65 Hadith 113 to justify the use of violence.

practices are a disguise, for their hearts are filled with hatred and fury against Islam."[44] Later, he goes further to assail these Muslims as *"Munifikun"* or hypocrites, saying that "Allah not only forbids us from electing the hypocrites as leaders, but Allah also forbids the believers from offering prayers for the dear hypocrites and from standing at their graves to offer prayer."[45] *Berjihad* is equally notable for the fact that it does not mention the spectre of global jihadi struggle that so pre-occupies many Muslim militants and terrorists today, nor does it allude at any point to the anti-Western and anti-Zionist motivations that capture Islamists and jihadists worldwide. In fact, it does not even comment on Muslim suffering and persecution elsewhere in the *ummah*. Thus, even in its highly polemical and ideological form, the points of reference in *Berjihad* are specific, narrow, exclusive, and local.

Many references to scripture belie the political poignancy of the document; the author makes it very clear that his objective is the liberation of Patani and creation of a separate state. Even the question of the Islamic character of this new state and the implementation of the *shari'a*, receives mere passing mention and appears secondary to this overarching objective. Unlike the highly ideological *zeitgeist* of Abdu Ala-Maududi and Sayyid Qutb, the author of *Berjihad* was not interested in delving to any substantive depth into the titanic struggle between Dar Al-Islam and Dar Al-Harb (as articulated by global jihadists), nor was he overly concerned about the alleged global threat posed by the *Jahili* to Islam, even though this is alluded to at a few token junctures without any further elaboration. The sole concern of *Berjihad* is, in its own words, the liberation of our beloved country from the disbelievers' occupation. In fact, much effort is made to rekindle memories of the valiant struggle of the Malay-Muslim "freedom fighters" and "jihad warriors" of a previous generation who fought and died for the same political cause.

The final chapter tellingly provides a systematic exposition of the executive and

---

[44] Ibid., 8.

[45] Ibid., 9. Note that according to an insurgent interviewed by the author, during a meeting of the leaders in charge of cells in several districts the matter of whether Muslim members of the Thai security forces were to be considered "munafiq" (Muslims who are outwardly religious, but are in fact unbelievers in their hearts) was debated. It was agreed by these leaders that this was not to be the case. Interestingly, the insurgent interviewed opined that the majority felt that if they had condemned Muslim security officials in this manner, it would have undermined their struggle. In his words: "it would be the end of our movement." Insurgent interview, Pattani, 14 March 2008. That said, the insurgent was not able to explain if this meant that Muslim security officials were thence not legitimate targets for attack.

legislative elements of the Patani state that would be established after the ejection of the "colonialists." Of particular interest is the fact that the "rightful" leader of the new state of Patani is envisaged to be "a royalty related to the Sultan of Kelantan."[46] This speaks not only to the historical ties that Malay-Muslims shared across the Thai-Malaysian border, but also to the reinstatement of what is in effect a historical kingdom that would transgress the present boundaries of southern Thailand and northern Malaysia. By focusing on Malay ethnicity and culture, the document effectively contravenes one of the fundamental tenets of Islam – that the faith supplants tribal identities and ties.

Berjihad is also notable for its attempts at amplifying latent antagonisms within the Muslim community in Thailand, exemplified by the author's use of *takfir* (the highly-politicized exercise of labelling fellow Muslims as infidels often associated with radical Salafis and Wahhabis), and blatant calls for the martyrdom fighters to Muslims deemed as hypocrites or unworthy. Indeed, the document reserves its most virulent attacks for members of the Muslim elite who have been co-opted into the Thai state. At one point, the author also disparages the practice of veneration that is often associated with Shi'a Islam, though not exclusive to it.

Finally, it is worth pointing out that there is a Sufi influence blended throughout *Berjihad*. In fact, despite Sufiism's relative unpopularity in southern Thailand, many of the religious rites associated with the 28 April attacks bore the imprint of militant Sufism seen previously in Chechnya, Sudan, Morocco, and Algeria. Numerous reports spoke of how the militants had engaged in practices such as the use of prayer beads, holy water, and "consecrated sand."[47] This connection with mysticism is further supported by the fact that Abdulwahab Datu, headmaster of Tarpia Tulwatan Mullaniti Islamic School in Yala, informed security officials during interrogation that he had been acquainted with the author of *Berjihad* (Poh Su Ismail), but subsequently distanced himself because he questioned the latter's belief in and employment of supernatural powers.[48] References to Sufi beliefs are also contained in the *Berjihad* document itself, particularly in relation to physical invincibility.[49]

---

[46] *Berjihad*, 24.

[47] Report of the Independent Fact-Finding Commission on the Krue Se Incident, released on 24 April 2005.

[48] "Imam admits to contact with separatists," *The Nation*, 1 September 2004.

[49] For instance, at one point the author writes: "We Muslims, who believe in Allah and the Prophet, never rely on modern weapons. It is an obligation for us to hope for Allah's help For He

The Internet

In addition to the beliefs of religious scholars and the pieces of literature described above, the internet is relevant to determining perceptions of the conflict in southern Thailand.

While the web has been a major arena of propaganda and indoctrination for terrorist ideology and political violence in recent times, most of the internet-based discussions of this nature have revolved around developments in the Middle East and South/Central Asia. To that end, conflicts at the margins of the Muslim world (such as Thailand and the Philippines) often get only token mention. This little attention is driven by calls for Muslims to be cognizant of the oppression that their co-religionists confront elsewhere. The exception is Indonesia and Malaysia-based jihadi websites, which frequently issue calls for Indonesians and Malaysians to join in the struggle to liberate Patani Darussalam.

In this regard, alarm bells sounded across regional counter-terrorism circles when a web posting appeared in late August 2008 on al-Ekhlaas, a known web-based jihadi forum. The post was purportedly made by an unknown group claiming to be based in southern Thailand, the Mujahideen Shura Council in Southeast Asia, which declared intentions to "begin operation under the name of 'Taubah operation' in the month of Muharram 1430H."[50] What captured international attention was the group's pledge of allegiance to Usama bin Ladin and Ayman al-Zawahiri, as well as its attempt to rebrand the conflict in southern Thailand from one solely based on Malay nationalism to an important facet of transnational jihad.

A major component of the web posting was an interview conducted by Khattab Media with Shaykh Abu Ubaidah, who claims to be a member of the Tandzim Al-Qa'ida Bahagian Asia Tenggara (Southeast Asian Division of Al-Qa'ida). In the course of the interview, Shaykh Abu Ubaidah argues that the historical conflict in southern Thailand has been "contaminated" by the spirit of nationalism (*masih terkena racun-racun nationalisme*), but since the 4 January Narathiwat arms raid and the 28 April Krisek Mosque incident (both in 2004), the conflict has taken on hues of a religious struggle or jihad to free the land from

---

is the only One who has weapons that are most powerful and have the greatest capabilities"; and elsewhere, "If Allah is willing, a rain of bullets could not harm us." See *Berjihad*, 7 and 17.
[50] As of 11 June 2009, the postings are still active at http://seruanjihaddipattani.blogspot.com and http://pattanidarussalam.blogspot.com.

Buddhist colonialism supported by the United States. Only when the mujahid of Patani realise this transformation will the struggle be bestowed with divine blessings and succeed.

Not surprisingly, the posting prompted a great degree of speculation as to whether a new jihadi operation had surfaced in Southeast Asia, and whether the violence in southern Thailand was about to spread beyond the erstwhile geographical confines of the three southern border provinces. Equally unsurprisingly, opinions were mixed among specialists; some expressed skepticism and saw the postings as nothing more than a "publicity stunt," while others took the declaration to mean that insurgents were about to take their struggle to Bangkok.

The August 2008 announcement also bore a striking resemblance to a declaration that surfaced earlier on a now-defunct website, Muharridh, in November 2005. The Muharridh posting was a declaration of war in Southeast Asia in which Thailand was specifically mentioned as a locale for violent jihad. The posting was written under the name Majlis Syura Mujahidin Islam (Al-Qa'ida Devisyen Asia Tenggara or Mujahidin Islam Shura Council)–Al-Qa'ida Southeast Asia Division. Tellingly, the name of this group bears close similarity to the name of the group responsible for the August 2008 post. Moreover, the August 2008 posting carried a list of signatories, including one Shaykh Abu Okasha al-'Arabi, Amir of the Shura Council, at the top. The November 2005 declaration was signed off by Abu Ukkasyah al-Arabi who described himself as the Supreme Commander of the Council. Again, the close similarity in the names is worth noting.

The declaration posted on Muharridh was more general and longer than the one posted on al-Ekhlaas. While the latter specifically targeted Thailand, the former threatened Southeast Asia in general, but with mention of specific countries. The 2005 declaration was divided into four parts: the first comprised of threats made to the governments of Thailand, the U.S., and their allies; the second part of the proclamation was an ultimatum to Malaysia and other "evil" Muslim governments; the third was a request for further instructions and weapons directed to Usama Bin Ladin and Ayman al-Zawahiri; and the last section appealed to Muslims in the region to stand up to the injustices committed against them. The references to Thailand include accusations against the Thai government for orchestrating terrorist acts that were then blamed on Muslims, and concluded: "The ummah in Fatani [sic] yearns for a sovereign Islamic government. Hence, their jihad against the Thai army is obligatory and praiseworthy." As alluded to earlier, perhaps what was most disquieting aspect of the posting was the claim of religious justification of violence. Citing At Taubah 29, the posting averred that a war has to be declared on those who do not worship Allah, those who are too concerned with worldly matters, those who do not forbid what has been forbidden by Allah and His prophets, and those who do not practice the Islam as defined by the fundamentalists.

The posting also cites the popular surah Al-Anfal 39, which calls for war to be waged against infidels until there is no more discord and Allah alone is worshipped. Nevertheless, the posting inevitably also made references to local history when it described the southern provinces as lands that belonged to Islam, and described the liberation of these lands as the responsibility of Muslims within the vicinity, a clear allusion to Indonesia and Malaysia.

After both the 2005 and 2008 postings, attacks and killings continued unabated in southern Thailand. That said, operations have remained confined to the southern border provinces. The calls in these postings aside, there is still no conclusive evidence of international jihadi presence or influence in the south. Indeed, large-scale terrorist activity has noticeably reduced over the last few years. It is important to note too, that the established insurgent groups like PULO and BRN-C have roundly rejected these postings. This is not surprising, given the fact that these groups are cognizant that any move on their part to cooperate or even communicate with international jihadi and terrorist organisations would fundamentally undermine their cause and objectives, and jeopardise the goodwill that they have cultivated in the international community (by playing up the human rights abuses perpetrated by Thai security forces). This is particularly true if they become listed as terrorist organisations. Indeed, the Jemaah Islamiyah and al-Qa'ida brand of religiously-sanctioned violence cuts little ice with the highly-localized and nationalist objectives of the southern Thai insurgency, which include greater political participation, recognition of Malay-Muslim identity and religion, the use of Jawi as the official language in the three southern border provinces, and greater control over economic resources in the region. This probably explains the general absence of transnational jihad narratives, which do not appear to have made a significant mark on the trajectory of the conflict.

The Salience of Jihadi Ideology in Context

From the preceding discussion, several observations can be drawn. First, there is a lack of published literature in southern Thailand in the genre of Islamist ideologies that espouse violence. Thus far, only two sustained articulations of the religious referents to the ongoing conflict – one oblique (*Jihad Sabillilah*) and the other overt (*Berjihad di Pattani*) – have surfaced in the theatre, thereby possibly indicating the lack of exegetical underpinnings to the conflict beyond general calls to "jihad." Of note is the relative lack of reference to the writings of Sayyid Qutb, viewed by many as the standard bearer of Muslim militancy, in the southern provinces. Indeed, while Qutb's *Milestones* has been translated for Thai consumption, this was done by the Young Muslim's Association of Thailand (YMAT), one of the most popular, government-sanctioned Muslim organizations in the country. Moreover, the translation was done, curiously enough, in Thai and not Jawi, thereby paradoxically limiting its accessibility in the southern provinces.[51]

Second, insofar as ideological underpinnings have been articulated and/or penned, they have been locally generated. In southern Thailand, armed jihad, the clarion call of Muslim militants, is referenced in terms of local conditions rather than broader themes, such as the Dar al Islam/Dar al Harb conflict. The books investigated above were written in Jawi (the local Malay language), and in the case of *Berjihad di Pattani*, the discussion is confined to the historical kingdom of Patani Darussalam. Third, insofar as the struggle is made with religious referents, they are both Salafi and Sufi in theological orientation. In turn, this is further indicative of: (1) absence of any sort of theological coherence or overarching religious ideology; and (2) a rather disparate character to the insurgency, which includes religious and nationalist elements, and even within the religious group there are differences.

---

[51] The following remarks were those of a member of the YMAT Advisory Council who was describing the misperceptions on the part of the Thai government towards the inspirational contribution that *Milestones* allegedly made to Thai Muslim society: "They [the Thai government] only wanted to see the militant side of Qutb and his language of revolution. But we saw a moral message in his work. The Thai authorities didn't understand that Qutb's work was a response to the problem in the Arab society. We, on the other hand, were not interested in carrying out a revolution. We are a minority, religiously speaking, in this country. The Arab Muslims were the majority in the Middle East and his message was in response to their predicament. We don't view ourselves as some immigrants coming here to profit from the land. In other words, we don't challenge the notion of the Thai nation-state. We are just trying to carry out work to ensure the continuity and strengthening of our community in Thailand." Interview with Saravud Sriwan-nayos, Bangkok, 27 May 2008. For a study of transnational Islamic networks in southern Thailand, see Joseph C. Liow, "Local Networks and Transnational Islam in Thailand," in *Transnational Islam in South and Southeast Asia: Movements, Networks, and Conflict Dynamics*, (ed.) Peter Mandaville et al., NBR Project Report (Seattle, W.A.: The National Bureau of Asian Research, 2009).

It is also important to moderate the terrorism analysis community's focus on the purported Wahhabi role in fomenting conflict in Thailand's restive south. To be sure, there are ultra-orthodox and conservative segments in the Malay-Muslim community of southern Thailand who have imbibed creeds often associated with the Wahhabi brand of Salafism. The presence of such teachings in the erstwhile traditionalist and Sufi-oriented southern provinces is a cause for concern in terms of pluralism in Muslim Thailand. There is, however, little evidence that Thai "Wahhabis"—as locals have also taken to calling these Muslims who challenge traditional Islamic practices—are involved in the insurgency. In point of fact, available evidence points to the contrary, namely, that the "Wahhabis" have been the most vocal critics of the insurgency and the use of violence.

Finally, notwithstanding religious allusions, references to ethnic identity are never far from the surface. More than anything else, this speaks to the culturally and historically rooted nature of this conflict. To be sure, the Malay-Muslims of the border provinces are keenly aware of developments in the larger *ummah*, particularly in reference to the oppression that their co-religionists are viewed to be suffering from the Middle East to Mindanao. Certainly too, there is not insignificant traffic between southern Thai Malay-Muslims and their co-religionists either through the internet, through educational networks, or even through the Hajj. All this means that southern Thailand cannot be easily insulated—at least not physically —from Muslim narratives, whether or not pertaining to violence, with a global reach. At the same time however, the Malay-Muslims in southern Thailand have proven to be extraordinarily resistant to foreign ideological influences upon their culture and religion. Indeed, even the Wahhabi community, mentioned above, has found it difficult to penetrate local society.[52] Whether a consequence of a strong sense of pride in the region's history as Southeast Asia's traditional centre of Islamic learning (somewhat misplaced, one could suggest, since beyond the shores of Pattani this is a history long since forgotten), inertia on the part of the local Muslim community to advance its knowledge of religion, or plain cultural chauvinism, the fact of the matter is that in an increasingly interconnected and globalized world, the conflict in southern Thailand remains remarkably insular in character.

---

[52] This is discussed at length in Liow, *Islam, Education, and Reform in Southern Thailand* and Joseph Chinyong Liow, "Religious Education and Reformist Islam in Thailand's Southern Border Provinces: The Roles of Haji Sulong Abdul Kadir and Ismail Lutfi Japakiya," *Journal of Islamic Studies* (forthcoming).

Conclusion

Given the increasingly popular use of religious metaphors by Muslim extremists today, it should not be surprising to find that Muslims engaged in conflict in southern Thailand make regular references to religion in an attempt to legitimize their struggle, enhance their appeal, and reinforce the sense of obligation among current and prospective fighters. To that effect, this chapter certainly does not claim that religion has no role in informing violence in the southern provinces. Such a view would be naïve; yet to suggest that what is taking place in southern Thailand is at heart a religious conflict would be an equally naïve and erroneous caricature.

Context is crucial in understanding the violence and conflict in Thailand's restive southern border provinces, and any reference to the influence of jihadi literature must be considered not solely for its exegetical value, but also for its usefulness in repackaging grievances into a narrative that provides further meaning and intelligibility for its consumers. Regardless of the extremist jihadi ideas that may or may not be circulating in the conflict terrain of Thailand's southern border provinces, to get to the heart of the problem one had to focus on the fundamental "root causes." For the insurgents themselves, these include: cultural and ethnic identity, historical accountability, and the perceived absence of justice.

A Survey of Southeast Asian Global Jihadist Websites

Jarret Brachman

Introduction

Jihadist websites aimed at winning the hearts and minds of Muslims have become pervasive over the past decade. These websites offer venues for jihadist minded individuals to disseminate material and discuss a variety of issues related to the jihadist movement. Although the sites differ in terms of quality, focus, or format, they each share and advance a common set of assumptions: first, jihadist websites are almost uniformly grounded on the premise that there is a global conspiracy to destroy Islam; second, these websites promote the argument that this conspiracy is being directed by the "Zionists" and "Crusaders" and administered by governments across the Islamic world who have failed to implement *Sharia* law in their respective countries; third, the sites seek to publicly demonstrate to Muslims that there is a vanguard of committed fighters who are actively resisting this global assault in the name of the entire religion.

Building on these common assumptions, jihadist websites advance the idea that groups like al-Qa'ida need more support from like-minded Muslims around the world who are willing to help their cause. Indeed, it is for these reasons—to catalyze support, mobilize the base, and expand awareness of this global resistance campaign—that jihadist websites claim they exist. They are designed to entice, inform, and rally Muslims to join in the fight to safeguard Islam. While the overwhelming majority of these sites are in Arabic and appeal to hard-line, Arabic speaking Muslims living in the Middle East, there are a growing number of jihadist websites appearing in other languages, including English, French, and German. These non-Arabic websites generally repeat the talking points found on the primary Arabic sites, rather than offering novel content into the global jihadist sphere. At the same time, however, an increasing number of sites are dedicated to fomenting jihadist sentiments in regions outside of the Middle East.[1] For instance, there is now a small but potent jihadist internet subculture within

---

[1] According to a report issued by the Australian Strategic Policy Institute, the levels of global jihadist websites, blogs, and their supporter websites in Southeast Asian languages is steadily increasing. Anthony Bergin, Sulastri Bte Osman, Carl Ungerer, and Nur Azlin Mohamed Yasin, "Special Report Issue 22 - Countering Internet Radicalisation in Southeast Asia," *Australian Strategic Policy Institute,* 6 March 2009,
http://www.aspi.org.au/publications/publication_details.aspx?ContentID=202&pubtype=-1.

Southeast Asia. The raw number of users on these websites is comparatively small in relation to the overall number of Muslims in the region. Yet a careful review of the activity on some of these websites suggests that those who frequent them are dedicated, if not fanatical, in their beliefs.

In some cases, the jihadist websites directed at Muslims in Southeast Asia serve as an alternative avenue for participation in the global jihadist movement, short of physical violence. In other cases, the sites may offer jihadist terrorist groups in the region an increasingly viable avenue to sustain their movements in an environment of heightened security. Finally, because the websites constantly seek to extend the sphere of potential new recruits and ideological converts, their growth in the region helps stoke the fire of jihadist ideological enlistment by reinforcing a core set of grievances and offering a violent set of solutions. In short, the websites can help propel ideological followers of jihadism closer to action.

This chapter provides an introduction to the topic of global jihadist internet activity in Southeast Asia.[2] Specifically, it concentrates on identifying the major

---

[2] Notably, no internet monitoring organizations in the West focus on Southeast Asian jihadist websites exclusively and few even cover those websites in their reporting. The leading work in this area has been done by Sydney Jones at the International Crisis Group. For a list of Sidney Jones's work, see her biography page on the International Crisis Group homepage: http://www.crisisgroup.org/home/index.cfm?id=1349&l=1. Her most directly relevant article on the transmission of global jihadist literature into the Southeast Asian context is: Sidney Jones, "International Influences on Jihadist Movements in Indonesia," *International Crisis Group* (May 2006). Jones has pioneered new ground by examining *Jemaah Islammiyyah* websites vis-à-vis more mainstream Arabic-language jihadist forums. She found extensive coverage by these Southeast Asian sites of classically Arabic jihadist figures, including the preeminent Jordanian jihadist cleric, Abu Muhammad al-Maqdisi; the legendary founder of al-Qa'ida, Abdullah Azzam; and the early jihadist instigator and author, Sayyid Qutb. One good indication of Jones' authority in this field is the fact that *Ar-Rahmah* recently issued an attack-piece against her. The article, posted on the *Ar-Rahmah* website, mocked her, called her a spy, and criticized her knowledge of the Indonesian jihadist movement. *Ar-Rahmah*, "Books Written by Mujahid Martyr Trio 'Selling Like Hotcakes,' Sydney Jones is Furious,"16 March 2009, http://www.arrahmah.com/index.php/news/read/3641/buku-goresan-pena-trio-mujahid-laris-manis-sidney-jones-sewot. The reason that Jones likely angers *Ar-Rahmah* so much is that her work makes the extent to which Indonesians jihadists use their websites to distribute the writings of their Arab counterparts clearer than others had to date. And perhaps more importantly, she identified that even though the writings of Arabic language jihadist scholars are available to anyone who wants to and can read them, local factors will tend to determine how those texts are used. In other words, bringing Arabic texts into the Southeast Asian region requires local expertise to identify, translate, and contextualize the works.

global jihadist media and online forums appealing to Islamists from Indonesia, Malaysia, and Thailand. It also seeks to understand the kinds of content that appears on these forums and how it compares to the content found on more traditional, Arabic-language global jihadist websites. There are two counterintuitive conclusions borne out by this chapter. The first is that one of the most significant influences on Southeast Asian jihadist websites, particularly blog sites, is a website run by a young, American jihadist propagandist. Samir Khan, the administrator of the website *Ignored Puzzle Pieces of Knowledge* and a contributing producer of *Al-Fursan Media,* is one of the most frequently cited propagandists on Southeast Asian jihadist websites.[3] The second conclusion is that jihadist websites in Southeast Asia are equally, if not more, focused on global jihadist issues than they are on local or regional issues. Even a cursory review of selected Southeast Asian websites demonstrates that the promulgation and translation of global jihadist media and writings in the region is a primary focus for these jihadist entrepreneurs.

Overview of Jihadist Website Activity in Southeast Asia

Only a small number of jihadist entrepreneurs in Indonesia, Thailand, Malaysia, and the Philippines promulgate most of the relevant online activity, but thanks to internet networks, the spread of their material transcends national borders and conventional understandings of time. Thus, jihadist material—be it books, videos, or essays—rapidly trickles down to the grassroots level. Indeed, wherever someone has a "connected" computer or cell phone, one can access a wealth of global jihadist material. Furthermore, the region's overall literacy rate is relatively high, which facilitates the successful distribution of jihadist material and activity on relevant blogs and web forums.[4]

At the same time, varying levels of technology diffusion rates complicates matters for these jihadist entrepreneurs. For instance, Indonesia—the world's fourth most populous nation with over 200 million inhabitants who are ethnically diverse, speak dozens of local languages, and live across 10,000 islands spanning thousands of kilometers—currently has the lowest level of internet diffusion among Southeast Asian nations, presenting an obstacle to jihadists

---

[3] *The Ignored Puzzle Pieces of Knowledge* website is available at http://revolution.thabaat.net.
[4] See http://www.unicef.org/infobycountry/. Indeed, the Indonesia postal service is an ISP in its own right, with some 20,000 subscribers. Ibid. Indonesia's total adult literacy rate in 2007 was 91 percent, according to statistics provided by the United Nations Children's Fund. Thailand has a 94 percent literacy rate. Malaysia sits at 92 percent and the Philippines is at 93 percent.

operating through websites. This obstacle will not last forever. In 2008, the Indonesian government unveiled a broadband rollout initiative, backed by NGOs, local businesses, international corporations, and the UN, that aims to provide 20 percent of the population with a cheap, fast connection via either wireless or mobile by 2012.[5] Furthermore, Indonesia has adopted the United Nations' target to ensure that 50 percent of the population receives internet access by the year 2015.[6] Meanwhile, other Southeast Asian nations are already relatively well connected. In 2007, the Philippines had 488 registered Internet Service Providers with 2.5 million internet subscribers.[7] In 2008, 44 percent of Malaysian households had direct exchange internet access lines with another 21 percent of households having broadband access, and nearly 97 percent of Malaysian adults had mobile phone access.[8] Moreover, even in places like Indonesia, internet cafes—or "Warnets," as they are called in Indonesia—provide a viable way for residents to access the internet. There are nearly 3,000 of these establishments operating around Indonesia. Indonesians may also access the internet from some one hundred post offices across the country.[9]

By examining the "blogrolls," or the links that one website will post to other websites, it becomes easier to understand where that website fits within the broader jihadist networks. In other words, by knowing who each site's administrators support, read, and promote, it becomes easier to triangulate their ideological positions and, potentially, sources of information and innovation. While most of the Southeast Asian jihadist websites include some reference to regional Islamic issues, they all advance the global jihadist ideology, particularly through their focus on the movement's classic laundry list of grievances, goals, and methods. It is also possible to track the root source of the blog postings that featured on many of these websites. Perhaps the most interesting of the trends seen across Southeast Asian websites is that much of the content is borrowed from *English-language* jihadist websites, rather than the premiere-Arabic language websites.

---

[5] See http://johnmill.wordpress.com/2008/08/01/digital-divide-1-the-bad-news/.

[6] Divakar Goswami, "LIRNEasia's WiFi Study in Indonesia Influences Policy Process," *LIRNEasia,* 14 October 2005, http://lirneasia.net/2005/10/findings-from-lirneasia-project-covered-by-indonesian-papers/.

[7] The National Telecommunications Web Portal, "Internet Service," http://portal.ntc.gov.ph/wps/portal/!ut/p/.cmd/cs/.ce/7_0_A/.s/7_0_EBH/_s.7_0_A/7_0_EBH.

[8] The Malaysian Communications and Multimedia Commission, "Facts and Figures," http://www.skmm.gov.my/facts_figures/stats/index.asp.

[9] Michael Minges, "Kretek Internet: Indonesia Case Study," International Telecommunication Union (December 2001), http://www.itu.int/ITU-D/ict/cs/indonesia/material/IDN%20CS.pdf.

Where most Southeast Asian websites seem to differ most from traditional Arabic-language jihadist websites is in their actual structures. Whereas the majority of Arabic jihadist online activity occurs by way of web forums, Southeast Asian sites tend to function more as hosted webpages, some even of commercial media organizations. Others appear as ad hoc blogs or amateurish attempts at homepages. This seems to suggest that there is a lower level of integration, coordination, and institutionalization among the respective websites and their administrators than is seen in Arabic-language websites. It also suggests that forums simply do not work in this region for structural reasons. With lower levels of technology integration and high popularity of internet cafes, many of the readers on these websites may be seeking news without the kind of time commitment or intellectual investment that a web forum takes. Indeed, on jihadist web forums, participants have to register their email addresses and set a password. If they post, they probably want to observe reactions to their post and possibly reply quickly to those responses. There are numerous sub-forums, each with tens if not hundreds of new posts per day. Tracking global jihadist forums, much less being an active member on these forums, takes significant amounts of time, commitment, and internet access. Finally, whereas the most elite Southeast Asian websites, like the Indonesian *Ar-Rahmah*, may have an organizational backer, most of the jihadist website administrators in the region have neither the professional staff nor organizational resources to grow their websites. In short, it is hard to say whether the aversion to web forum structure, which is the dominant website structure of Arabic-language global jihadist websites, is due to the fact that forum structures are simply not as popular in the Southeast Asian context or if the technical demand in hosting them and the labor it takes to participate on them has made them nonviable.

Global Jihad Online: Indonesia

Despite the technological diffusion rates discussed above, across Indonesia, there is a growing and vibrant jihadist discussion online. A number of Indonesian websites and media production houses focus local attention on a variety of issues that are of both domestic and global importance.

Ar-Rahmah

Indonesia's leading jihadist website, *Ar-Rahmah*, has 12,123 registered members and features 10,914 posts.[10] In this sense, *Ar-Rahmah* rivals the leading Arabic-

---

[10] Forum statistics gained from http://www.arrahmah.com/index.php/forum (accessed 23 April

language jihadist websites, which have similar numbers of members and posts. Thus, although *Ar-Rahmah* receives less coverage by internet monitoring groups and the Western media, it is operating on the same premiere level as the high priority Arabic jihadist websites. *Ar-Rahmah* is also the most sophisticated of the Indonesian jihadist sites in terms of its web design, as well as the most comprehensive in terms of offering original content with more frequency on diverse topics in a greater variety of languages.[11] The main website links include: "Forum," "Blog," "Local," "International," "Technology," "Jihad Analysis," "Interview," and the "English Section." What this expansive number of options for original and translated media content suggests is that the *Ar-Rahmah* organization has a robust staff of dedicated writers, web designers, and support staff to keep all of these components functioning. This kind of operation simply dwarfs most other jihadist websites today, including many of the Arabic-language sites.

Ar-Rahmah has become a multi-media production and dissemination force in recent years, making it a highly effective vehicle for the dissemination of global jihadist propaganda around Southeast Asia. For instance, it is known broadly as the production house of Abu Muhammad Jibril Abdulrahman, better known as Abu Jibril,[12] the deputy chairman of the militant group, Indonesian Mujahidin Council (MMI). A leading jihadist media operator, Abu Jibril has been imprisoned in both Malaysia and Indonesia on charges related to terrorism and extremism.[13] His organization, MMI, has partnered with *Jemaah Islamiyyah* (JI) and *Jamaah Ansharut Tauhid* (JAT), a new jihadist organization founded by JI's former leader, Abu Bakr Basiyr.[14] At the same time, *Ar-Rahmah* brings some of

---

2009).

[11] Most Arabic-language jihadist websites, including *Al-Faloja* and *Ana al-Muslm*, are exclusively forums. There have been some now defunct Arabic language websites that have sought to offer multiple formats of jihadist multimedia, including original media, news, streaming radio, a blog, and a forum. The most notable example of this was the now-defunct, *al-Tajdeed* website, which had been administered by British jihadist Muhammad al-Masaari. The fact is, however, that most Arabic-language websites do not have the number of options to engage.

[12] The *Jakarta Post* provides useful information about Abu Jibril. See, e.g., Tahil Ramani, Yogita, and Kartika C. Bagus, "Alleged al-Qaeda-linked network in Central Java," *Jakarta Post*, 26 January 2002.

[13] For more information about Abu Jibril and the Indonesian jihadist movement, see Zachary Abuza, "The Trial of Abu Bakar Ba'asyir: A Test for Indonesia Publication," *Terrorism Monitor* 2, no. 21 (9 May 2005); Zachary Abuza, "New Polling Data in Indonesia Shows "Significant" Support for Terrorists," *Counterterrorism Blog*, 15 October 2006, http://counterterrorismblog.org/2006/10/new_polling_data_in_indonesia.php.

[14] Tom Allard and Sunanda Creagh, "Tears Flow for Bali Victims," *Sydney Morning Herald*, 13

the most popular jihadist literature, video production, and imagery into the Indonesian public dialogue, making it accessible to audiences who otherwise might not be exposed to it. Some of these products are original, including analyses by the site's in-house "international jihad analysts," "M. Fachry" and "Prince of Jihad," but most of the products are repackaged from other production-outlets.[15]

In addition to having a sophisticated media dissemination function, *Ar-Rahmah* offers Indonesian Muslims a forum for discussion, education, and debate on par with any Arabic-language forum in terms of its formalization, aesthetic appeal, and amount of traffic. These web forums are qualitatively different from the unidirectional process of media consumption, as they offer a venue for dialectical interchange. Furthermore, it is operationally safer, in terms of monitoring by law enforcement, to communicate in a forum environment than via more traditional ways, including email. One can use anonymous proxy servers to log into these sites, never have to enter biographical information, and can send private messages to one another using the forum's internal mail program.[16]

Finally, *Ar-Rahmah* stands apart from many other jihadist media outlets because it aggressively and openly promotes itself as a legitimate organization. Its contact information is plainly published and updated, including a physical address, email address, phone number, and website URL.[17] In addition, the site contains numerous announcements about upcoming Islamic book fairs to which it will be

---

October 2008, http://www.smh.com.au/news/national/tears-flow-for-bali-victims/2008/10/12/1223749846309.html.

[15] For *Ar-Rahmah's* "International Jihad Analysis" section, see http://www.arrahmah.com/index.php/blog/analysis. Topics span the range of global jihadist issues including commentary on *As-Sahab* productions, the establishment of new jihadist organizations, the global financial crisis, the election of Barack Obama, jihadist response to the feminist movement, and more.

[16] Governments around the world find themselves in a predicament when it comes to managing jihadist websites. On the one hand, they offer an important window into the mindset, doctrine, debates, and media of the global jihadist movement. The continued operation of these websites can, therefore, prove valuable for law enforcement and intelligence collection activities. On the other hand, websites like *Ar-Rahmah* can produce so much content and reach out to so many people in a visually compelling way that the question must be raised whether it would be better for a government to close such a website for security purposes. Other complicating factors include domestic rights to free speech, which can offer protection to webmasters and administrators who are not overtly threatening governments, targets, or populations.

[17] Contact information is available by way of the *Ar-Rahmah* "Contact" page at http://www.arrahmah.com/index.php/contact/.

sending representatives to make their VCDs, books, and posters available for public purchase.[18] *Ar-Rahmah* has also been engaged in organizational outreach efforts. One of its most interesting cooperative relationship is with *Radio Dakta*, where *Ar-Rahmah* regularly airs sermons given by Abu Bakr Basir and Abu Jibril.[19]

There are very consistent themes advanced in the types of media hosted and disseminated by *Ar-Rahmah*. Although *Ar-Rahmah* does report on domestic political and Islamic issues, the website leans mostly toward issues involving the global jihadist movement. The site regularly links to articles from international media outlets including the *New York Times*, *Le Monde*, and even U.S. government official reports.[20] The Forum section is highly active, populated with new threads and regularly posted responses, much like any of the major Arabic forums. Sub-forums include a section dedicated exclusively to *Ar-Rahmah* media products, as well as "Jihad News," the "Islamic World," "Women and Jihad," and numerous other topics. Notably, however, there are relatively few postings and replies when compared to the total number of registered members on the website. This dissonance between the high numbers of registered members and low numbers of posts, reads, and replies can be explained by the fact that members might be simply more interested in the other kinds of content. This trend seems consistent with the fact that among Southeast Asian jihadist websites, at least anecdotally, blogs seem to be more popular than web forums.

Ar-Rahmah's "Blog" section includes postings about a variety of topics and produces a new blog approximately every four days. The organization's staff tends to focus almost entirely on issues related to the global jihadist ideology as opposed to issues of immediate local or parochial concern. Some of the most recent blog posts included discussions on: Usama Bin Ladin's statements; a profile of the mid-twentieth century Egyptian jihadist thinker Sayyid Qutb;

---

[18] Numerous posts at the *Ar-Rahmah* forum discuss the presence of *Ar-Rahmah* media representatives at book fairs and bazaars around Indonesia and Malaysia. Some of the threads that include these discussions are:
http://www.arrahmah.com/index.php/forum/viewthread/1059/;
http://www.arrahmah.com/index.php/review/read/3501/angin-surga-dari-ar-rahmah-media-novel-jihad-petama-di-dunia; and
http://www.arrahmah.com/index.php/news/read/3518/dimana-stand-ar-rahmah-media.
[19] "Prince of Jihad," *Jihad Magz,* http://www.arrahmah.com/index.php/news/read/1631/jihad-magz-membumikan-jihad-merealisasikan-syariat.
[20] Western media sources pervade the analyses contained in the *Ar-Rahmah* "International" section, which can be found at http://www.arrahmah.com/index.php/news/international.

updates about the al-Shabaab jihadist organization in Somalia; and even analysis of the formation of the jihad in East Turkestan.[21] This global focus of the *Ar-Rahmah* blog would be, more than likely, dictated from the *Ar-Rahmah* leadership, given the highly organized and calibrated approach that its website seems to take. The absence of blog posts on local or regional issues suggests either that such issues are being discussed elsewhere on the website, that the site administrators do not view local issues as being compelling to the readers, or are themselves not interested in discussing them. Either way, the finding is counterintuitive given the local nature of many conflicts ongoing in Southeast Asia.

Ar-Rahmah's "Local" section is the only section on the website that focuses specifically on political, religious, and social issues in Indonesia and the region.[22] The topics discussed the most include local elections, trials of regional Islamic terrorists, the inefficacy or hypocrisy of local governments, and apostate Islamic groups operating in the region. The posts tend to feature color photos and refer readers to other posts on similar topics. The *Ar-Rahmah* "International" section concentrates mostly on exposing the crimes of the United States, Israel, and the Arab governments, commonly identified as the global jihadist movement's enemies.[23] In addition, this section highlights the accomplishments of the global jihadist movement. This approach again fits squarely with the media strategy employed in Arabic language jihadist websites. The *Ar-Rahmah* "Technology" section presents news stories about advances in technology or its application that might be of relevance to a jihadist audience.[24] Interestingly, most Arabic language jihadist forums have sub-forums on technology within their discussion forum section, but very few have a narrative and analytical technology section such as this one.

Ar-Rahmah has identified a number of enemies through their products and website. Many include the usual enemies of jihadists, including the Muslim Brotherhood, HAMAS, and other more mainstream Islamist groups. Others are less obvious to non-Indonesia specialists. The website is particularly upset with a

---

[21] The *Ar-Rahmah* "Blog" section can be accessed at http://www.arrahmah.com/index.php/blog.

[22] The *Ar-Rahmah* "Local" section can be accessed at http://www.arrahmah.com/index.php/news/local.

[23] The *Ar-Rahmah* "International" section can be accessed at http://www.arrahmah.com/index.php/news/international.

[24] The *Ar-Rahmah* "Technology" section can be accessed at http://www.arrahmah.com/index.php/news/technology.

group named Al-Qiyadah al-Islamiyah that the Indonesian government, through the Majelis Ulama Indonesia (MUI), banned for its supposed deviance from Islam. *Ar-Rahamah* has taken repeated aim at this group.[25]

Perhaps the most aggressive and innovative multimedia effort by *Ar-Rahmah* has been its recent publication and dissemination of the online global jihadist magazine, JIHADMAGZ, which is available at <http://www.jihadmagz.com> .[26] Although there are numerous jihadist online magazines in Arabic and several in English, there are few in this region. The magazine's "About" page explains that its goal is to "make the world a better place."[27] It references several key global jihadist figures, including Abdullah Azzam, Shaykh Yusuf al-Uyayri, and 'Esa al-Hindi.[28] The identification of these figures helps to further place the website in the global jihadist, rather than Islamist or regional separatist, ideological camp. The magazine does not publish the names of its own local journalists or contributors, listing instead al-Qa'ida-linked or jihadist foreign media outlets as sources of its news. Some of these sources include *Al-Fajr Media* and *Al-Furqan Media* in Iraq; *As-Sahab Media*, *As Sumud Media*, and *Lee Media* in Afghanistan; *Kavkaz Center* in the Caucasus, Russia; *As-Shabaab Media* in Somalia; the website of American jihadist propagandist, Samir Khan; the *Al-Firdaws Jihadist Forum* (now defunct); and the English-language *Islamic Thinkers Society*. This eclectic combination of official and marginal global jihadist sources spanning several languages suggests that the magazine's editors are open to innovation and content from diverse sources. In other words, they seem to accept that many different outlets may offer useful insights and ideological direction. What seems to be occurring here, on a more tactical level, is that the magazine uses the global jihadist media outlets —major multimedia releases, including speeches, statements, interviews, and videos— for broad ideological direction and content. Anecdotal review of content suggests that the magazine's editors fill their jihadist knowledge gaps by drawing on the commentary and analysis of the English websites. This lends further credence to the fact that these English jihadist websites have more influence than likely assumed because they help to shape the nature of the conversation and analytical focus of organizations like *Ar-Rahmah*.

---

[25] For a list of twelve articles dating from 27 October 2007 to January 2009 on *Ar-Rahmah*, see http://www.arrahmah.com/index.php/search/results/6f571b1abb80fe3eabe5974d37e19c0f/.
[26] "Prince of Jihad."
[27] See http://www.jihadmagz.com/v1/profil.html.
[28] Ibid.

The magazine, having published at least three issues between June 2008 and March 2009, also carries articles profiling numerous global jihadist figures, including: Taliban leader Mullah Muhammad Umar; Supreme Leader of the Islamic Caucasus State, proclaimed in Chechnya on 31 October 2007, Dokka Umarov; Supreme Leader of the Islamic State of Iraq, announced in October 2006, Abu Umar al-Baghdadi; the Palestinian-born jihadist ideologue during the Soviet occupation of Afghanistan, Shaykh 'Abd Allah 'Azzam; and the American al-Qa'ida member, Adam Gadahn. The magazine also hailed the creation of the Al-Qa'ida Organization in the Islamic Maghreb following the merger of a local jihad group known as the Salafist Group for Preaching and Combat and al-Qa'ida elements. Furthermore, the magazine profiles "enemy literature," including the Combating Terrorism Center at West Point's publication, *The Militant Ideology Atlas*.[29] What makes these references worthy of discussion is that they are archetypal of the global jihadist movement, both in the kinds of authors that they respect as well as those that they fear. Thus, these references further support the argument that the banner publication for the *Ar-Rahmah* media house is a *global* jihadist publication meant for local consumption, not a regional or local publication.

Other Indonesian Jihadist Websites

Beyond *Ar-Rahmah*, there is a vast array of other Indonesian jihadist websites. None of these others can compete with the formalization or commercialization of *Ar-Rahmah* in terms of structure and format. They do, however, follow a consistent model in terms of content. The content across these lower-tier websites can be grouped into five basic categories: local and regional jihadist concerns, profiling enemies of global jihadism, celebrations of jihadist attacks, the state of the global jihadist movement, and the religious ideology of global jihadism.

It is difficult to assess the total number of Indonesian jihadist websites currently in operation. An anecdotal survey suggests that there are no more than forty websites, but it is likely that significantly less than forty are being regularly updated.[30] Some of the other leading Indonesian jihadist websites operating at the time of this writing include:

---

[29] The reference to the Combating Terrorism Center's *Militant Ideology Atlas* was made in the second JihadMagz issue, released 1 June 2008 on the *Ar-Rahmah* website as well as in print. The *Atlas* can be found at http://www.ctc.usma.edu/atlas/.

[30] A more comprehensive list of historic and current Indonesian jihadist websites would also include the following: http://www.geocities.com/abuya_2005/almuhajirun;

- *Al-Muhajirun* (http://www.almuhajirun.net/)
- *Muslim Daily* (http://muslimdaily.net)
- *Musadiq Marhaban* (http://musadiqmarhaban.wordpress.com/)
- *InfoJihad* (http://infojihad.wordpress.com)
- *My Khalifa* (http://www.mykhilafah.com)
- *Al Ghuroba* (http://ghuroba.blogsome.com)
- *Syaheeda-Islamic Distro* (http://Komunitas-distro.blogspot.com)

Al-Muhajirun describes itself as the "voice, eyes and ears of Muslims" and claims that it is not just a website, but rather an "Islamic movement" that is dedicated to fulfilling the Qur'an and Sunnah. The website graphically projects a dark, imposing image, featuring a solid black background with old English styled text in the banner. It also maintains its own logo, which is designed with high-resolution graphics. The structure of the website is broken down into several basic categories, including "Links," "Contact," "Book," "Mailing List," and "Sawt ul-Islam Bulletin." While considerably less comprehensive than *Ar-Rahmah*, *Al-Muhajirun* maintains an extensive archive of blog postings, which span a range of topics. The blog itself uses the following posting categories, which help to give an insight into the thematic focus of the site's administrators: "Tawhid," "Manhaj," "Sharia," "Adab," "Nisa," "Jihad," "Afghanistan," "Iraq," "Kashmir," "Caucasian," "Palestine," and "Somalia." Again, the lack of a major global jihadist web forum attached to the website is peculiarly Southeast Asian. In the Arabic-language global jihadist world, a website is not significant (with the exception of some repository websites like Abu Muhammad al-Maqdisi's library, *Tawhid.ws*), unless it has a discussion forum structure. In Southeast Asia, the prevalence of websites like *Al-Muhajirun* suggest that global jihadist websites are situated somewhere between formalized news websites and blogs are the preferred, or at least dominant, structure.

The *Muslim Daily* website is another content-rich extremist Indonesian jihadist Islamist website. Like other Indonesian sites, it is structured around a menu of several sections, including: "Home," "News," "Articles," "Opinion," "Women's," "Interview," "Consultation," "Special Features," and "Journalist Release." Again, there is not any sort of robust discussion forum embedded within this website. Rather, it functions more along the lines of a global jihadist

---

http://members.tripod.com/darul_islam/; http://www.voiceofimaan.net/; http://www.asy-syahadah.com/; http://www.bawasel.asy-syahadah.com/index.htm; http://www.boemi-islam.com/index.php; http://www.boemi-islam.com/old/head.html; http://www.hidupdialamjihad.2ya.com/; and http://swaramuslim.net/ebook/index.php.

news, information, analysis, and blog website. Readers can come to the website, download certain content, and leave. There is little dialectical back-and-forth involved in the process, as there might be on a web forum page. There are two significant differences between the *Muslim Daily* website and *Ar-Rahmah*. The first is that it has a section dedicated to women, which highlights the particular role of women in advancing the global jihadist agenda.[31] Some of the articles featured in this section discuss the operational contributions that women have made; others focus on issues such as menopause, childbirth, and prostitution. The second significant difference on the *Muslim Daily* concerns the focus of their "Interview" section. Whereas *Ar-Rahmah's* "Interview" section is dedicated almost entirely to global jihadist figures, primarily senior al-Qa'ida members or regional al-Qa'ida commanders, *Muslim Daily's* "Interview" section profiles regional Islamic figures.[32] Furthermore, while each *Muslim Daily* profile deals with the interplay between Islam, politics, society, and violence in different ways, they all do so from an inherently local perspective.

Global Jihad Online: Malaysia and Thailand

There are significantly fewer Malay-language and Thai-language global jihadist websites than there are Indonesian-language sites. Moreover, none of the jihadist websites that do exist in these languages offer the same comprehensive coverage or original media that the *Ar-Rahmah* website does. This suggests that many of the leading global jihadist entrepreneurs in the region are either from Indonesia or particularly focused on Indonesian constituencies. This may be because of the entrenchment of local and parochial groups in Malaysia and Thailand, but this is more likely to be true in Thailand than Malaysia.

Malaysia

According to an article published by Reuters, the number of radical and extremist websites in Bahasa and Malay rose from fifteen in 2007 to 117 in 2008.[33] Of those, traditional websites rose from ten to sixteen, while blogs and social networking sites rose from zero to eighty-two. Notably, there seems to be a strict separation between Malay Islamists, on the one hand, and global jihadists, on the

---

[31] For a list of articles on the *Muslim Daily* website that are dedicated to women, see http://www.muslimdaily.net/cari/0/wanita.

[32] *Muslim Daily's* "Interview" section is accessible at http://www.muslimdaily.net/wawancara.

[33] "Internet seen a growing weapon in Asian radicalization," *Reuters*, 10 March 2009, http://www.canada.com/topics/technology/news/gizmos/story.html?id=52aaa99c-4933-449d-8471-068ef22994eb.

other. The former are busy pursuing parochial agendas through violence or resistance activity, whereas the latter are more focused on discussion, proselytizing, and media efforts. One Malay global jihadist website that receives attention across the region is *Patanikini* <http://patanikini.wordpress.com>.[34] Structurally, the *Patanikini* website is very low-tech, with virtually no graphics, designs, or formatting upgrades from the base Wordpress on which it was designed. The site has been in existence since March 2007, and since its first two years in operation it has logged 37,000 total visits.[35] Other than the fact that *Patanikini's* list of links to other websites, or "blogroll," includes a number of global jihadist websites, there are no features or amenities to the website worth noting.[36] In fact, perhaps the most anomalous attribute of the website is its minimalist quality. In terms of its content, *Patanakini* seems evenly split between promoting southern Thailand as a key front in the global jihadist movement and promoting the global jihadist agenda itself.

There are at least two reasons for the lack of prominent global jihadist websites in Malay. First, a significant amount of jihadist energy tied to Malaysia is by way of Indonesian jihadist entrepreneurs. Recent reports show a gradual influx of Malay-language jihadist material in the form of books and other "hard" channels, but there are few Malay-language websites that remain relatively unsophisticated.[37] This suggests that Malay-language jihadist media may be produced and imported from the outside. The second reason relates to the influence of outwardly non-violent Islamist groups operating in Malaysia, like *Hizbut Tahrir Malaysia* (HTM).[38] HTM is the Malaysian chapter of the pan-Islamic global movement and self-proclaimed "liberation party," *Hizbut Tahrir*.[39] This

---

[34] For example, participants like "Ghurabaa" reference postings and media on the *Patanikini* website in the *Ar-Rahmah* forum,
http://www.arrahmah.com/index.php/forum/viewthread/511/#2385.

[35] The founding date of the Patanikini website was obtained from the first month of archived posts: http://patanikini.wordpress.com/2007/03/.

[36] Websites included in *Patanikini's* blogroll include Amandamai - propaganda siam (http://www.amandamai.com/ - now defunct); Harakahdaily (http://www.harakahdaily.net/); Patani News (http://www.pataninews.net/ - in Thai and English); Propaganda Penjajah (http://www.topix.net/th/pattani - English language); Sejarah Perjuangan (http://www.terasmelayu.net/sejarah_perjuangan_melayu_patani.htm - now defunct); utussan-patani merdeka (http://utussanpatani-merdeka.netfirms.com/ - Malay language news website).

[37] "A Growing Terror Threat," *Straits Times*, 6 March 2009.

[38] See http://www.mykhilafah.com/.

[39] For an English summary of Hizb ut-Tahrir's positions and global structure, see, http://www.hizb.org.uk/hizb/index.php. For an example of how the various HT movements promote one another, see this article about Hizb ut-Tahrir Malaysia on the Hizb ut-Tahrir United

group expends most of its resources and energy in proselytizing, preaching, and educating. Its focus is "Caliphatist" in that its long-term goal is to establish Islamic rule globally. The group is not, however, jihadist in the sense that it believes the best way to accomplish the establishment of a global Islamic caliphate is through the immediate use of violence, revolution, or insurgency. HTM's website, <http://www.mykhilafah.com/>, is composed almost entirely in Malay, although it does maintain a regularly updated English section. It has an ostentatious banner and graphical presentation. In terms of content, the website focuses on the establishment of the global Islamic Caliphate, hosting a small repository of Caliphatist articles, all of which are tracked in terms of the number of downloads by the website, and some of which have received thousands of hits.

The high number of hits on HTM's website suggests that these more mainstream Islamist or non-violent revolutionary groups may have more sway and popularity in the Malaysian context than extremist, pro-violent groups. The lack of any robust global jihadist organization in Malaysia, at least when compared to Indonesia, is probably the byproduct of broader cultural and national trends. It suggests that Malaysia is more likely to import jihadist content and media of Indonesia.

Thailand

Thai-language jihadist websites do not seem to be as corporatized as Indonesian websites in their presentation. Rather, many of the Thai sites reviewed for this chapter seemed structured around an informal network of blogs and personal websites. Similar to Malay-language jihadist websites, Thai websites concentrate more on steady streams of reporting presented in less organized formats. *Baitulansar's* website <http://baitulansar.wordpress.com>, entitled "Sons of Tawhid and Jihad," is representative of the new generation Southeast Asian jihadist websites, as it relies on template-based software (Wordpress), it makes heavy use of Youtube video clips, high-gloss graphics, and dense links to other pages.[40] As of March 2009, the site had registered over 5,300 hits since its inception just two months earlier. This number suggests that the site has a steady, yet relatively low-level stream of visitors. Its graphical banner features the Islamic State of Iraq's black flag and the profile of a little-known member of

---

Kingdom chapter website: http://www.hizb.org.uk/hizb/who-is-ht/a-global-party/gaza-hizbut-tahrir-malaysia-handed-over-memorandum-to-malaysian-armed-forces.html.
[40] *The Sons of Tawheed and Jihad* website can be found here: http://baitulansar.wordpress.com/.

al-Qa'ida's High-Command, Abdallah Sa'id, who appeared in the 8 February 2009 *as-Sahab Media* release of "Winds of Paradise III," a documentary-style video that focuses on the lives of individual mujahidin and glorifies martyrdom.[41] The decision to profile this individual is confusing, as he is not a well-known figure to the global jihadist movement. He does seem, however, to be a senior member of al-Qa'ida focused on operational aspects of that group's mission, possibly transitioning to a more prominent media role. By using his graphic, perhaps the *Baitulansar's* website administrators are suggesting that they are trying to bridge the operational and media worlds, much like Abdallah Sa'id seems to be doing.

The "About" page of the *Baitulansar* website explains that it will "not tolerate" the situation of its fellow Muslims.[42] Because of the deluge of false media reports and deception campaigns launched by the enemies of the global jihadist movement, the website suggests that Muslims must be careful in who they look to for guidance and news. One trusted source, according to this page, is Samir Khan, whose blog, *The Ignored Puzzle Pieces of Knowledge*, is supposed to offer the kind of truth and inspiration that Muslims today desperately need.[43] This focus on Khan's website, not just as another link on a "blogroll," but as a page that receives explicit praise for its veracity and dedication on a prominent Thai language jihadist website is of analytical interest. It suggests, above all else, that an American self-styled jihadist propagandist is influencing the direction of at least a portion of the Southeast Asian global jihadist websites in terms of the content that they cover and the analytical lines that they adopt on a variety of positions.

Baitulansar's blog aims to accomplish three tasks. First, it seeks to restore spiritual love and knowledge of *Sharia,* which is necessary because, in his view, Muslims and their leaders have abandoned the teachings of Allah. Second, the blog commits itself to reporting on global jihadist military operations with the goal of "reflect[ing] reality and uncover[ing] the lie and deception of the unbelievers," targeting hypocrites and authoritarian governments.[44] Finally, the blog aims to provide "news to the believers" and to "offend the enemies of Islam (those who attack Islam with their arms, tongues, assets, property, etc…)."[45]

---

[41] The Winds of Paradise III video, released by the *As-Sahab Media Establishment,* can be accessed here: http://www.archive.org/details/winds-of-heaven-3.

[42] The "About" page can be accessed here: http://baitulansar.wordpress.com/about/

[43] *Ignored Puzzle Pieces of Knowledge.*

[44] See http://baitulansar.wordpress.com/about/.

[45] Ibid.

In terms of content, the blog posts reflect interest in a variety of global jihadist topics. Consider the blog's debut post topics on a randomly selected, yet representative, day (20 January 2009): there is a link to a Youtube video of a wedding reception where Shaykh Abu Muhammad al-Maqdisi was in attendance and a written blog text about the waning Islamic commitment from Muslims in Southeast and East Asia. Abu Muahmmad al-Maqdisi is a preeminent global jihadist ideologue and scholar, thus his presence on a Thai-language jihadist blog clearly fits with the global focus of the administrators. What makes the video so interesting, however, is that the link originated from, according to the website itself, Samir Khan's *Ignored Puzzle Pieces of Knowledge* website. Khan's site also served as the resource for the *Baitulansar* blog's link to an al-Fajr assassination video, as well as a link to Shaykh Attiyattallah's book, "American Criminals Caught and Engaged in a Dirty War." The fact that Khan's website populates media content for a Thai-language jihadist website is, like *Baitulansar's* positive reference to Khan's site, a significant factor that remains underappreciated.

Other postings on the selected day included a Thai-language post with photos highlighting American domestic dissent regarding the war in Iraq. This is a good example of how the administrators are able to take a global jihadist enemy, the United States in this case, and argue that it is weakening due to domestic political instability, but do it in a local language and interpret it as a victory for local efforts. It is this confusing and often irrational integration between global ideology and local constituencies that Southeast Asian websites have been perfecting in recent years.

Alistishhad <http://alistishhad.wordpress.com/> is another Thai-language global jihadist blog. It has not been updated since January 2009, but has been in existence since July 2007, and has over 23,800 hits since its inception.[46] On its "About" page, composed entirely in Thai, it states: "We believe that there are many problems in society and even the Islamic world today. The origin of those problems have come from the same source… not applying the government and laws of Allah. This blog and all its content is [sic] dedicated to abandoning human laws and establishing the divinely inspired laws of God on Earth."[47] The structure of the *Alistishhad* site is typical for a self-styled jihadist website. It posts

---

[46] The website URL is: http://alistishhad.wordpress.com/. Its founding date can be identified by examining the first month of the website's "Archive" section, which is available here: http://alistishhad.wordpress.com/2007/07/.

[47] See http://alistishhad.wordpress.com

on current events, new al-Qa'ida media releases, links to articles, books, *nasheeds*, and offers a variety of links to other jihadist websites. The blog categories include: "Afghanistan," "Al-Hadith," "Al-Quran," "Announcements," "Aqeedah wal Eman," "As-Sahab," "As-Sirah wat Ta'rikh," "Books," "Boycott," "Chechnya," "Da'wah," "Documentary," "Ibadah," "Iraq," "Jahiliyah," "Jihad," "Muslimah," "News," "Pakistan," "Palestine," "Salaf as-Saleh," "Ukuwah," and "Waziristan." These categories reveal several things about the blog's focus. First, there is ample attention paid to the theological and religious dimensions, not just political aspects, of the global jihadist movement. This focus also suggests that the website administrators have some religious knowledge and prioritize religion as an element equally important to the physical waging of violent jihad. The categories also suggest that the administrators prioritize certain regions in the global jihad, including: Afghanistan, Chechnya, Pakistan, Palestine, and Waziristan. What is most revealing about this list is not what regions are featured, but which ones are not. Specifically, there is no reference to Saudi Arabia, Jordan, Egypt, Yemen, or North Africa. Although there is no reason given for the focus on some regions over others, it suggests that jihad is only of interest to this website in particular countries.

The jihadist books featured on *Alistishhad* are divided into two sections, Thai-language and English-language. The Thai books are primarily hosted on the website <http://www.iqraonline.org>, which is the Society for Online Learning, a Thai-language Islamic literature repository and web forum. None of the texts would be considered among the preeminent jihadist texts. This focus on more local Islamic literature contrasts from the Indonesian and Malaysian websites reviewed in this chapter, most of which herald global jihadist literature written originally by the chief jihadist thinkers in Arabic. The English language jihadist texts, on the other hand, do include those authored by some of the most well-known jihadist writers, including Sheikh Bin Baz, Sayyid Qutb, Abdullah Azzam, Sulayman ibn Nasr al-Ulwan, Aid al-Qarni, Nasr al-Deen al-Albani, Hasan al-Banna, and others. None of the English language books deal with local or regional issues, and the list of authors constitute a veritable "who's who" list of Arab jihadist thinkers.

This breakdown between English and Thai-language texts leads one to draw at least two conclusions. First, there seems to be a relatively even split in the website's focus between local/regional jihadist issues and global jihadist issues, although this divide does not extend to the action arena. Rather, the Thai-language focus on jihadist ideology seems almost entirely focused on the practice and understanding of Islam, not the engagement of violent jihadist activities. The second conclusion is that there is no effort to translate global-focused Arabic-language jihadist literature into Thai. The website's interest in promoting these books in other languages, however, suggests that this trend may not continue into the future.[48]

Conclusion

Historically, Southeast Asian jihadist internet entrepreneurs have played only a minor role in the global jihadist online movement. Websites emanating from this region receive comparatively less traffic than their Arabic jihadist web counterparts. Most of these websites offer little novel content, parroting the style and substance of the more conventional Arabic- and English-language websites. At the same time, the Southeast Asian site structures tend to be more ad hoc in nature and built around blog formats as opposed to web forum formats.

What is perhaps most intriguing about Southeast Asian jihadist websites, particularly those in Indonesia, is that many of them use lower-level English jihadist websites as their inspiration. This influence can be seen in three ways. First, some of the websites actually identify particular English language jihadist websites that they use as their inspiration. One website that anecdotally seems to hold a substantial amount of sway over these websites is Samir Khan's *The Ignored Puzzle Pieces of Knowledge*. What makes his website so useful to non-Arabic speaking jihadists in Southeast Asia is that it distills the deluge of jihadist media into the most important releases and offers candid commentary on contemporary issues. In a way, Khan's website functions almost like a news wire service might for the websites, offering them the jihadist equivalent of content, news feeds, and stock analysis. Given that it is in English, it is likely more accessible to Southeast Asian jihadists than the premiere Arabic websites might be. This observation is further supported by the fact that virtually no website reviewed in this study linked to any of the prominent Arabic jihadist web forums.

Second, the "blogrolls," or lists of links included by Southeast Asian websites, link to more lower-level English language jihadist websites than to other Thai, Malay, or Indonesian websites. While this reflects little formal coordination across Southeast Asian websites, it does suggest that there seems to be self-organizing or guiding principle drawing these sites to common inspiration.

---

[48] The author is happy to provide a more complete of Thai websites sympathetic to Salafi perspective upon request.

Viewing the Southeast Asian jihadist web world as a learning, adaptable, decentralized, and ideational network might be a better approach than thinking of it in organizational terms. In other words, even though most jihadist web administrators in the region are likely not coordinating in any formal way, they are probably learning from one another's content and style, tracking one another's links, perhaps even inspiring and influencing one another. Furthermore, they have seemingly found a proxy for direct consensus or organizational coordination by mutually linking to English-language jihadist websites. When multiple Southeast Asian jihadist websites "peg" their site's approach to common anchors, in this case several English-language jihadist websites, then they will reflect commonalities even if they never coordinate amongst one another.

As much as Southeast Asian jihadist web entrepreneurs would like to transform the region into an integral part of the overall jihadist web world, there are few indicators to suggest that this will happen any time soon. The level of participation and the overall sophistication of the conversations generally pale in comparison to other areas. More importantly, there is a clear directionality at work here: Southeast Asian websites receive from, rather than give to, the global jihadist movement. There are no indicators that these websites are having any impact on the global jihadist dialogue, nor does it seem as if they are actively trying to shape that discourse. This reality does not, however, mean that these websites are irrelevant. Southeast Asian jihadist websites are currently in the midst of finding their proverbial legs. The administrators of these sites are discovering what types of content resonates with their target audiences, as well as learning web design, graphics design, and technological skills. Moreover, they are already regularly drawing in thousands of viewers to these websites. It will only be a matter of time, all things remaining equal, before the Southeast Asian region develops a more robust and dynamic jihadist online community.

About the Contributors

Dr. Greg Barton joined Monash University as the Herb Feith Research Professor for the Study of Indonesia in January 2007, based in the school of Political and Social Inquiry (PSI) in the Faculty of Arts. Prior to that he had worked as an Associate Professor at the Asia Pacific Center for Security Studies (APCSS) in Honolulu, Hawaii, where he continues to teach counterterrorism courses as an adjunct professor, and before that at Deakin University. At Monash Greg is Director of the Centre for Islam and the Modern World (www.arts.monash.edu.au/politics/cimow) and Deputy UNESCO Chair in Interreligious and Intercultural Relations – Asia Pacific. He teaches undergraduate and postgraduate units on the politics of the Muslim world. He also teaches and researches in the field of counterterrorism and has a deep interest in comparative politics. Greg has written or edited five books and published dozens of refereed articles and book chapters in this field. His biography of Abdurrahman Wahid, *Muslim Democrat, Indonesian President: A View From The Inside*, was published in 2002; *Indonesia's Struggle: Jemaah Islamiyah and the Soul of Islam*, was published in 2004. He is currently working on two other book projects: Progressive Islamic thought and social movements in Indonesia and Turkey and *Islam's Other Nation: Faith in Democratic Indonesia*.

Jarret Brachman is a specialist on jihadist thought and propaganda. He routinely advises the U.S. military, intelligence and law enforcement agencies on those issues. Brachman also directs a new program in counterterrorism and security policy at North Dakota State University's Upper Great Plains Transportation Institute. Brachman has testified before the House Armed Services Committee, spoken before the British House of Lords and his research is regularly cited in international press. His recent book, *Global Jihadism: Theory and Practice*, was published in 2008 by Routledge Press.

Professor De Castro is currently the U.S. State Department ASEAN Research Fellow from the Philippines and is based in Arizona State University as an adjunct faculty of the Political Science Department (January to July 2009). He is also on the faculty of the International Studies Department (on sabbatical leave) and the holder of the Dr. Aurelio Calderon Professorial Chair of Philippine-American Relations. He received his Ph.D. from the Government and International Studies Department of the University of South Carolina as a Fulbright Scholar. He is the author of several articles on international relations and security that have been published in a number of scholarly journals and edited books in the Philippines, Malaysia, Singapore, South Korea, Taiwan,

Germany, the United Kingdom, China, Canada, and the United States. He can be contacted at decastror@dlsu.edu.ph.

Rohan Gunaratna (Ph.D. St Andrews) is head the International Centre on Political Violence and Terrorism Research and Professor of Security Studies at the Rajaratnam School of International Studies, Nanyang Technological University, Singapore. He was a former Senior Fellow at the United States Military Academy's Combating Terrorism Center and at Tufts University's Fletcher School for Law and Diplomacy. He interviewed detainees in Afghanistan, Pakistan, Bangladesh, India, Sri Lanka, Iraq, Philippines, Indonesia, U.S. and several other countries. As a litigation Consultant for the U.S. Department of Justice, he testified in the Jose Padilla case. He is the author of a dozen books including *Inside Al Qaeda: Global Network of Terror* published by Columbia University Press in New York.

Scott Helfstein is an Assistant Professor in the Department of Social Sciences and an Associate at the Combating Terrorism Center at the United States Military Academy at West Point. He has provided terrorism policy advice to the U.S. Department of Defense and briefed Special Operations Command on various aspects of terrorism. His work has appeared in *Public Administration Review*, and has forthcoming articles in *Studies in Conflict and Terrorism* and *Nonproliferation Review*. Scott completed a Joint Doctorate in Political Science and Public Policy at the University of Michigan in 2008, where he majored in world politics. He also earned a Master's Degree in War Studies from King's College London in 2004. From 1999 to 2002, Scott worked as an investment banker focusing on mergers and acquisitions at Credit Suisse First Boston. Prior to that, he worked at the Federal Reserve Board of Governors in the Banking Supervision and Regulation and Research and Statistics Divisions from 1997 to 1999. Scott also holds an undergraduate degree in finance from the George Washington University. Currently, his research addresses terrorism, nonproliferation, networks, decision making, and grand strategy.

Joseph Chinyong Liow is Associate Professor and Associate Dean at the S. Rajaratnam School of International Studies, Nanyang Technological University, Singapore. His research interests are in the themes of Muslim politics and international politics in Southeast Asia, and intrastate conflict. His most recent publications are *Islam, Education, and Reform in Southern Thailand: Tradition and Transformation* (Institute of Southeast Asian Studies, 2009) and *Piety and Politics: Islamism in Contemporary Malaysia* (Oxford University Press, 2009).